Drugs: Losing the war

Issues in Social Policy

Drugs
Losing the war

Colin Cripps
with cartoons by Barney Cripps

New Clarion Press

First published 1997

New Clarion Press
5 Church Row, Gretton
Cheltenham GL54 5HG
England

New Clarion Press is a workers' co-operative.

A catalogue record for this book is available from the British Library.

ISBN   paperback   1 873797 20 6
        hardback   1 873797 21 4

Typeset in 11/13 Times by Jean Wilson Typesetting, Coventry

Printed in Great Britain by Bookcraft (Bath) Limited

Contents

Preface

This book is a collection of thoughts about what I believe are the main issues for drugs policy and drugs work at the present time, focusing particularly on the experience of my own agency, the Newham Drugs Advice Project in London.

It does not attempt to be a definitive guide to illegal drugs, although it examines the major drugs in some depth. Neither does it attempt to be a comprehensive history or social policy review, a practitioner's guide or pharmacology; but it does attempt to ask the right questions and to explore the interaction between all these elements that makes the 'drugs issue' such a complex, involved and seemingly intractable one. It includes pointers for those working in the field on how I believe practice can be improved, and raises dilemmas that we all need to face in our societies.

Thanks to Louise and my whole family for their support throughout, and to Viv, Mal, Ruth, Lee, Steve, Jo, Abdul, Jib, Carlo, Danny, Sunil and everyone else at the Newham Drugs Advice Project and Youth Awareness Programme, who constantly provoke me with ideas, questions and inspiration.

Colin Cripps

1

Camouflage

The war on drugs is a bar-room brawl. Or perhaps it is a civil war, a guerrilla war like Vietnam. What it is not, is a clear-cut fight between two sides, good and evil, where everyone has their battle lines clearly drawn and knows who is on their side.

In fact, calling it a war at all has hampered our responses to a complex issue to such a degree that every new initiative, every positive step forward, is distorted to the point where it becomes nearly unworkable. Everything is reduced to good guys and bad guys, to a series of untenable stereotypes. Every idea is co-opted to support the 'fors' and 'againsts'.

If this is a war, then we're losing it. And we're all going to suffer for it.

We're losing the chance to tackle the real problems that drugs can cause because those who take the important decisions, the policy makers and the funders, often know little about drugs or drug users other than that which they get from the media. They are left to draw on the same old pool of stereotypes.

And the media? Well, a war on drugs is just great by them. A war gives you sensational headlines; calm, rational responses to matters of complexity do not. The media define the language and the debate, the language governs the thinking, the thinking defines the policy responses and we're suddenly in Disneyland.

Politicians and policy makers run scared and play safe for fear of being labelled 'soft on drugs'. Anyone who sticks their head above the parapet gets it blown away – ask Labour front-bencher Claire Short, who was jumped on by the press and her own party leadership merely for suggesting that we should have a debate about legalizing cannabis. Debating is a war-crime; it is the action of a traitor. But it is not merely in the debate about legalization of drugs that terror rules and safety comes first. In every area of policy we are able only to inch forward, always defining new initiatives in terms of the past or, more commonly, regurgitating old initiatives which have repeatedly failed. This works on every level of decision making, from the Cabinet to the District Health Authority purchaser.

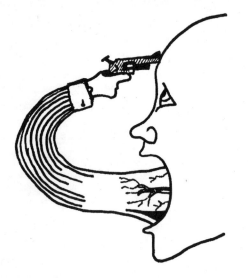

Encouraging an open debate

Diplomacy

For all its faults, 'Tackling Drugs Together', the UK government drugs strategy put together in 1994–5 under the guidance of Tony Newton, then Lord President of the Privy Council and Leader of the House of Commons, was the bravest and most pragmatic attempt so far to move forward. But although the ideas it contained were couched in carefully media-safe language, it did not prevent both the policy and the man being given an undeserved savaging by a vicious press.

I was present at the press conference to mark the first anniversary of the strategy, and witnessed the ferocity and vindictiveness of the media response. The idea of presenting young people with credible information about drugs, so that they could make informed choices, was mauled as 'telling young people that drugs can be a good thing. You've given up fighting and given in to damage limitation.' The Home Secretary at the time, Michael Howard, immediately, shrewdly and in keeping with his right-wing credentials responded by changing the meaning of 'informed choices' to 'the choice between right and wrong'. Tony Newton was quizzed about his own daughter's cannabis use, and it was suggested that perhaps he hadn't brought her up properly. Over the previous few days a booklet on drugs, produced by the government for parents, was attacked by the media as 'making drugs sound like a good thing', merely for giving parents information about those effects of each drug which were perceived by users as desirable, as well as giving them information on their dangers. The Prime Minister, John Major, responded by delivering a speech full of every possible stereotype and distortion, in order to re-present his party as 'tough on drugs'. It was a speech which had nothing to do with the strategy whose anniversary we were there to take note of.

Similarly, in drugs education, teaching packs are endlessly produced and posts advertised, supporting models of drugs education which have failed again and again to reduce levels of drug use among young people, to slow down the rate of increase, to reduce the damage to young people's health or to attract more young drug users to treatment services. Why do we repeat them? Because they're not controversial. They make the adult world feel safe that the professionals are in control. Most important of all, they aren't going to land anyone on the front pages of the newspaper under nasty headlines.

Treason

The old adage goes that the first casualty of war is truth. In wartime, a press that is supposed to represent freedom of speech becomes a propaganda machine, and truth becomes treachery.

So let's commit treason. Let's ask a few basic questions. Who says this is a war? Who are the opposing sides? What is the battle really between? Because, after all, we're really only talking about a range of chemicals that have certain effects when taken by humans, and it's pretty difficult to fight chemicals. What is more, nearly all of these chemicals have played a role in medicine at some time: Queen Victoria took cannabis for period pains; GPs used to prescribe amphetamines as slimming aids; cocaine was hailed by Sigmund Freud as a 'wonder drug' that would transform the lot of the human race; LSD and ecstasy were used in psychotherapy; heroin was and is used in pain relief. The list goes on. No, you can't wage a war against chemicals. Chemicals are neutral. It is how they are *used* that attaches value or values to them. The war on drugs is a war between people and ideas.

In reality there is a spectrum of views about drugs, from those at one end who believe in abstention from all mind- or mood-altering substances (including legal ones like alcohol), to those at the other end who believe that it is the right of the individual to take whatever they want provided they don't hurt other people.

This spectrum from time to time places wildly different groups close together: the old International Socialists (IS) insisted on abstention from their membership just as the *Daily Express* regards drug use as a moral crime. In both cases the drugs were representative of wider ideas. For IS, the vanguard of the revolution had to have clear heads in order to analyse correctly the strategies of the class war. Drugs were symbolic of decadent consumerism, used by capitalist society to distract the working class from the call to revolution. For the *Daily Express*, drugs are symbolic of the moral decline of our society, of youth on the rampage and out of control. Hedonism is anarchy is the end of social order.

At the other end of the spectrum, similar strange rubbings of shoulders can be found. The libertarian left by and large follows in the philosophical footsteps of Timothy Leary, originator of the International Foundation for Internal Freedom, by insisting on the right of the individual, in full knowledge of the risks, to put whatever substance they wish inside themselves providing they don't harm others. (Interestingly, the possession of drugs is a victimless crime and one which has a 100 per cent clear-up rate because the offence is only committed if the offender is found with the drug in his or her possession.) Such thoughts find favour also in certain areas of the far right: drug use can be seen as a simple matter of individual responsibility and market forces.

Even on a philosophical level, this is not a straightforward political battle between right and left. If this is a war then both sides contain some very interesting regiments!

On closer scrutiny, few of the ideas held at the extremes of the spectrum hold up. Those who regard the use of illegal drugs as a moral issue, a choice between right and wrong, cannot do so on the grounds of health or hedonism because most exclude legal drugs such as alcohol from their arguments. Alcohol is clearly potentially extremely damaging to health and encourages some of the worst extremes of violent and anti-social behaviour. What other drug has users who are only dimly aware of the presence of other users lurching around the streets in fighting mood on Saturday nights, shortly before they vomit on the pavement! This is not representative of an objective moral stance; it is a subjective reaction to what many see as a disintegrating society. They want things to stop now before it all collapses; the way to stop things is to ban them. Alcohol use, on the other hand, represents a traditional way of life and is therefore okay.

The libertarian argument is just as full of holes. First, if a substance alters our perceptions or moods, it must alter our behaviour. Taking drugs would otherwise be pointless. If our behaviour is affected, we must affect others. Drugs are not taken in a vacuum, they are taken in social situations. If individuals are changed by substances, so is society.

You may be able to take pharmaceutically pure heroin every day of your life and remain a fully functioning member of society, but the same cannot be said of 'crack' cocaine. It is in the nature of the drug that its consumption is likely to get out of control, and prolonged use will undoubtedly change personality and behaviour. Whether legal, pure and freely available or not, crack will pose a problem not only for the user, but also for those around them.

The argument for all illegal drugs to be freely available also contains another contradiction. Many of its supporters would be among those complaining of the pharmaceutical industry putting drugs on the medicines market that have not been properly tested. Modern medicine is littered with drugs which have turned out to be a liability, from thalidomide to barbiturates. In fact, the drugs that are currently illegal nearly all became so as a result of problems identified with their use as medicines. Are we really going to argue for the free availability of all substances, tried and tested or not? Many problems with drugs do not surface for some time. We are at present going through a major social health experiment with ecstasy, and there are already some disturbing signs for the future.

Confusion

To every legitimate philosophical position on drugs there is a counterview with just as much strength. In pragmatic terms, dealing with drugs is not a simple issue and we should not pretend that it is. The mistakes we can make by doing so can have far-reaching consequences. Alcohol provides a salutary example: the prohibition of alcohol gave an enormous boost to organized crime from which the USA has never recovered; an argument, you might say, for legalization. The relaxed licensing laws in France, however, allowed greater consumption of alcohol than in the UK and correspondingly higher rates of cirrhosis of the liver. Interestingly, the UK has, in recent years, relaxed the licensing laws and increased the penalties for both the supply and possession of illegal drugs.

Time for more basic questions then. Why and when are drugs a problem, and for whom? If we are 'Tackling Drugs Together', what is it that we are tackling? Until we define the problem, we cannot begin to reach the solution.

Many would argue that the consumption of mood-altering substances is a basic aspect of human behaviour. Certainly there is evidence of such substance use in every society and culture since the dawn of time, whether this behaviour was prohibited or not. What is this relationship between human and substance founded upon, which gives it such a hold?

In today's modern western consumer society, it is often very difficult to begin to pick out the roots of why people behave as they do. Drug taking is often seen as pathological or deviant behaviour, as a self-medicating response to a traumatic life, as a disease, as the result of a personality defect, as the outcome of a lack of self-esteem. Such patterns of drug use are not, however, the mainstream. They may represent the behaviour patterns of a minority of problematic drug users; they do not portray the motivations of the vast majority of young people, in particular, who take drugs.

Another time, another place

Before we look at the motivations of today's young, we need to get a wider geographical and historical perspective which we can use as a framework for understanding. If we look at the ways in which drugs have been and are used in other cultures, past and present, we come across yet another set of complexities.

Drugs which alter perception or mood have been held in reverence by a wide variety of religions for thousands of years. In Christianity, wine is symbolic of the blood of Christ; but in many beliefs it is the experience of taking a drug which gives the drug its spiritual value.

Hallucinatory or 'psychedelic' drugs have played a part in both ritual and personal spiritual experience in many cultures. The fly agaric mushroom has been used for its hallucinatory properties across much of the northern hemisphere, including Siberia where mushroom eating was a communal activity. Mescalin, found in the peyote cactus, was used by Native American Indians. In one sense, the reason that these plants were afforded such status is easy to see. If you believe that life exists on other planes beside the one we normally experience – the dream world, or nirvana, or the spirit world – then it is easy for such drugs to seem like a door to those worlds. They certainly transform our experience of the world around us to such an extent that for many people reality will never seem the same again. When you have seen the world as a different place, the degree to which the mind governs our interpretation of experience becomes all too clear. If reality is liable to different perception, what is reality? What are we? What is this universe we live in?

We can see the effect of hallucinatory drugs on belief systems if we look at youth culture in the late 1960s and 1970s. The use of LSD transformed popular art and music; *Sergeant Pepper* and *Axis Bold as Love* could not have been made without it. The drug was instrumental in opening up youth culture to beliefs and value systems from Asia and the Orient. The establishment was right to see its use as a threat to traditional values and beliefs. Even those who didn't take it felt its social shock waves. The language surrounding LSD at the time was the language of exploration of learning and of spirituality. The expressions used at the time seem quaint and dated nowadays – 'turning on' and 'tuning in', 'cosmic oneness', 'expanding the mind', 'far out', 'spacy' and so on – because, although the use of the drug continues, the experience of it has been assimilated into consumer society. Young people who use LSD nowadays don't talk of 'enlightenment' because to them LSD is just a chemical that changes the way things look and sound, and which makes crazy things happen. Quite revealing.

Other drugs have been used throughout time to improve or enhance performance. Such is the drug use of the cheat, in modern sport, but it was not always so. Andean Indians have chewed coca leaves to help them function at high altitude for centuries, apparently without harmful affect. Amphetamines have been given to soldiers in most recent wars to enable them to stay awake longer and to give them more energy. Indeed, it could be argued that amphetamines changed the course of history quite drastically. Adolf Hitler was given amphetamine by his personal physician in increasing dosages as the Second World War went on. Any 'speed freak' will identify the following behaviour: paranoia, plots imagined everywhere, a 'bunker' mentality; rash confidence and aggression coupled with increasingly poor and irrational decision making. Connections made?

Yet further substances have been used for relaxation. In our society and countless others, alcohol is the main relaxant. But in many cultures, cannabis has performed that function.

Here and now

Nowadays, the main reason for people to use drugs is to have fun. While there still exists the basic social desire to belong and therefore to behave in the same way as one's peers – the reason that nearly all smokers start smoking cigarettes – drugs reward initial experience with pleasure. The experience of adjusting perception and mood is most commonly a highly pleasurable one. Cannabis smokers will clutch their sides with laughter at apparently innocuous comments or events; they will enjoy profound and deeply significant conversations which they can barely remember two minutes later, let alone the next day. Ecstasy users will enter a world where their body has boundless energy and where their feelings of empathy and, indeed, love for others are overwhelming; a world without violence or difference; a brave new world of the moment and of the senses that mirrors the name of the drug. Cocaine and crack users will find themselves initially supremely self-assured and confident, sharp and on top of their game, quick-witted and with energy to spare. Heroin users will become cocooned from the pain of the world, both physical and emotional, outside and inside themselves.

We deny these perceived positive effects at our peril because they are both the main attraction and one of the main problems with drugs.

If this were the only side to the story, surely we would not see drugs as a problem at all and they would be freely available. I tend to think not. On a social and a spiritual level, societies have always regarded drugs with reverence, with caution and as potentially very dangerous – and for reasons entirely unassociated with health. The line between spiritual revelation and escape into other worlds is a fine one. Societies which have accepted hallucinatory drugs have not done so without restriction. Strong social and religious codes have governed their use, ensuring that they are not overindulged. An individual who regularly retreats from the world because a substance can take them to a cosier or a more exciting place is able to avoid tackling all sorts of problems and issues. Without facing those problems there is no personal growth; many people who have been dependent on drugs for many years find that, when they stop, old problems and old emotional responses reappear from before they started taking drugs.

We have a strong tendency as humans to return to and revisit pleasurable experiences. Given that drugs are such a pleasurable experience, it is a great temptation to continue returning to them for the reward they give. That's straightforward behaviourism. The more we repeat this behaviour and are rewarded, the more difficult it becomes for us to disassociate the activity and the result in our minds. As time goes by, this association can become so strong that we cannot get the result without the behaviour. In other words, if we turn to, say, cannabis to relax and find that it works, then when we want to relax it will be natural to return to cannabis. If it keeps working for us, cannabis and relaxation become almost synonymous.

Before long, we stop believing we can relax without cannabis. If we then have problems occurring in our lives that we find hard to deal with, it will be easy to use cannabis more and more of the time so that we feel able to 'cope' with the stress. If we are 'stoned' all the time, we can't function properly in society, which in turn creates more stress and more need to relax, and so on. That's not a good thing for us, and it is certainly not perceived positively by society. Slow, unmotivated people are not productive, and societies want active citizens who can be productive when there is a call for them to be so.

Another agenda

From the puritan and teetotal tradition of much British and US Christianity to the strict codes of Islam, the pleasure principle is viewed with mistrust. It is not, therefore, surprising that the hedonism of today's youth and drugs culture provokes such strong moralistic reactions. Where the heady blend of left-wing revolutionary politics and drug-inspired mysticism of sixties youth culture was perceived as a clear threat to social order by the establishment and most adults of the time, today's ecstasy-fuelled 'rave' culture has promoted an even heavier-handed response. New laws have been introduced, ostensibly to deal with the threat to the health of our nation's youth from the use of ecstasy in rave culture – draconian laws such as the Criminal Evidence Act in the UK. These laws clearly are not there for the stated reasons. If the health of youth were the issue, we would be clamping down on under-age smoking and drinking, or even on solvents, as they all kill far more people. Ecstasy and rave culture represent a far more basic threat to society than that. Young people in rave society are not revolutionaries, there is no new political idealism; they 'fight for the right to party'. They have taken consumerism to its ultimate and most threatening limit: they buy 'love and peace' in a pill; they don't attack 'straight society', they ignore it, because the drug allows retreat into a totally self-contained, if temporary and illusory, world. Now that's dangerous.

With health problems being held up as the justification for the 'war on drugs', it is natural that, to justify new laws and the virulence of the attacks on 'traitors', these health problems will have to be presented as pretty extreme. The most extreme health problem is obviously death, and it is therefore death on which the media concentrates and on which laws are introduced. The number of deaths directly attributable to drugs, however, is very small compared with those from alcohol and tobacco. I am not saying that deaths from illegal drugs aren't tragic and that we shouldn't do everything we can to stop them. What I *am* saying is that the parents of young people who die as a result of nicotine and alcohol grieve every bit as much, that there are a lot more of them, and yet they are invisible. On the other hand, parents of young people who die from ecstasy get immediate media coverage. Even where the cause of death is attributed to alcohol, if the young person took ecstasy as well, it will be the ecstasy which gets the headlines.

The reason for this is simple. If we want to create the impression that ecstasy is the problem, showing distraught parents brings the issue into the homes of ordinary people. Humans can't think on the grand scale. We can't imagine millions of people. To us the global village is just that. Mass communications distort the world to make it smaller. Those parents on our TV, in our living room, become people we know. Never mind that this is a comparatively rare experience; it could be the people next door, or us. If we don't see the parents grieving over the child who fell into the road drunk, it didn't happen. We know cerebrally from the occasional reporting of the statistics that 25,000 a year die from drink and 100,000 from cigarettes, but we haven't been touched emotionally by their deaths as we have by the grief of the parents of Leah Betts, whose ecstasy-related death made banner headlines in the UK in 1996.

The problem with such distortions is that young people know they're not the way things really are. They don't believe them and they are not scared by them. By creating such hysteria, we may easily pave the way for ever more intrusive laws and ever harsher penalties, and may aid the causes of the moral minority on the political right. But we may also be putting young people at greater risk by cutting them off from much needed truth and support.

Real risks

The irony is that there are a great many health problems associated with drug use which get ignored or distorted by those who feel pushed to 'defend' drugs as part of a wider battle of values and beliefs. Drugs are very poor territory to defend because there are undoubted major problems caused directly by their consumption. I will consider some of the health problems associated with particular drugs in more depth later in this book, but I am concerned here to lay out the territory in general terms, to look at the unseen and equally serious problems that drugs cause people, but which are overlooked in the fascination with death.

In terms of physical health, there is a list of problems caused either directly by drug use or by behaviour patterns associated with them. With the stimulant drugs such as amphetamines and cocaine, eating can be seriously disrupted, and drastic weight loss together with the symptoms of vitamin and mineral deficiencies can be a major concern. Drugs that are smoked, such as cannabis, can cause a number of respiratory problems. A carcinogen, cannabis is smoked without a filter and the smoke is held down in the lungs for longer than with an ordinary cigarette. While cannabis is regarded as a 'soft' drug in the terminology of relative harm associated with the battle for its legalization, it may ironically emerge in years to come as the greatest real killer of them all through lung cancer. The recent increase in cigarette smoking among the young may also turn out to have been caused by 'spliff' smokers being introduced to nicotine in this way.

Injecting drug use carries a number of major health risks. There is damage to the veins caused by the formation of scar tissue which reduces blood flow. There are sores and abscesses caused by unsterile injecting practices and, of course, there is the well-publicized link with the transmission of diseases like HIV and hepatitis.

Mental health presents another range of problems associated with drug use, especially with stimulants like amphetamines and crack cocaine, but also with hallucinogens such as LSD and ecstasy. I have worked with people who have not returned properly or at all from the LSD alternative universe – people who see colours glow and smear across their vision for months after a 'trip'. Others feel their sense of reality and thus their own basic confidence seriously undermined by 'acid'. I have worked with young people whose faith in the workings and sensations of their own body has been fundamentally disturbed by ecstasy use: with those suffering from debilitating panic and anxiety attacks, drastic and uncontrollable mood swings, depression and racing thoughts. I have worked with crack users who imagine vast and bizarre conspiracies against them, involving strange alliances of their friends, families and government agencies.

Then there are the accidents: those who drive while 'stoned' or on an 'E'; kids having accidents while intoxicated with aerosol spray cans.

Probably the most awful and degrading of all is the relentless round, for those who feel themselves dependent upon a drug, of craving, obtaining money, buying drugs and satisfying craving for ever-decreasing pleasure return. This is a seven days a week, fifty-two weeks a year problem for some. Being dependent on a drug is hard work; you don't get weekends and holidays off.

Then there are the problems that drug use and its associated behaviour can cause family and friends. There is the strain they can place on relationships: living with someone who has paranoid rages isn't a lot of fun; nor is living with someone who is too stoned to get out of the armchair. Cannabis use can undoubtedly affect young people's motivation to go to, or work at, school. It can affect their concentration, memory and co-ordination, so that learning is impaired.

Estimates of the amount of crime attributable either directly to drug use or indirectly to drugs as a means of finance tend to hover around 60–70 per cent. There is no doubt that in areas where crack has become a big problem – often the poorest areas, least able to afford such a problem – levels of acquisitive crime and shootings are very high. Some people take this as a sign that drugs should be legalized, thus bringing their price down, but that would not necessarily be the answer. If drugs were legalized (and they won't be), they would undoubtedly be taxed. When I was a youth worker, the most common criminal activity among the young people I worked with was breaking into off-licences and social clubs to steal legal cigarettes and alcohol.

Perhaps most overlooked of all, brought on partly by the drugs trade itself and partly by the policy responses to it, is the problem for minority communities and the effect on the economies and quality of life of developing 'producer' countries. The black community in the UK has long found itself stereotyped as pro-drugs, particularly cannabis and crack cocaine. This stereotype has allowed some extremely heavy-handed policing of black people and the areas they live in under the banner of the war on drugs. Attempts by black communities to deny a drugs problem have led them, in turn, to underreact to the spread of drugs, and have created the conditions, as in the white communities, which allow gangster culture to be imported lock, stock and barrel from the USA by their young adults.

Economic wars

Countries in South America, Africa and Asia became ensnared in the drugs trade by being led into debt by western banks in the 1970s, seeing commodity prices collapse soon after and then finding that their most sought-after and valuable produce was illegal drugs. Prices of commodities like sugar, coffee, wheat, tin, lead, crude oil and iron ore fell by between 17 and 64 per cent during the late 1970s and 1980s. In 1990, Latin American and Caribbean countries were $420 billion in debt.

Not that the drugs trade improved their economic situation very much. The cartels and criminal armies that ran the trade tended to launder the money abroad. In the informal currency exchange in Lima, Peru, $3 million change hands every day. Four-fifths of Bolivia's parallel currency market comes from coca, the plant from which cocaine is manufactured. In Colombia, the cartels gross $50 billion each year, but only $2–4 billion gets back into the Colombian economy. The rest is invested overseas or in western banks.

Peasant farmers still live, by and large, in poverty, forced by threat of violence to grow drugs instead of food, and subject to regular brutalization by government forces trying to stop the trade. They are the real losers in the drugs business.

In 1985, Bolivian farmers could earn $9,000 from growing 2.2 acres of coca, whereas 2.2 acres of citrus fruit would earn them only $500. Farm wages for growing coca are six to eight times higher than for other crops, but food is now in short supply because of coca production. Health problems are growing for those whose job it is to tread the coca leaves in kerosene during the conversion process to cocaine. Toxic residue from drugs manufacture poisons the rivers. Some 50,000 Bolivians have a cocaine problem. In Peru the figure for those with cocaine problems is 150,000, and in Colombia, 600,000. This is a drugs problem on a global scale.

Meanwhile the drugs trade turns over more each year than the oil industry, and has become the world's second largest area of activity after the international arms trade. It is now so inextricably linked to legitimate financial activity that it is hard to see how we could afford to eradicate it quickly, even if we had the means to do so.

The link with the arms trade itself is more than passing. Drugs mean big money, and money buys arms to fight real wars. During the Afghan war between the Soviet Union and the mujaheddin in the 1980s, much of the mujaheddin weaponry was bought with money from the production and sale of heroin and cannabis. The West found it in its own interests to turn a blind eye to this activity, since subsidizing the rebel armoury would have been a costly business. In the Middle East, the Bakaa valley in the Lebanon has long been an important area to control because of the cannabis grown there. Being in control of areas of drug production brings enormous power: officials, politicians, generals, financial institutions and even presidents can be bought with drugs money.

The drugs problem is a complex mix of issues. Health concerns, law and order, moral and social values, politics and global economic considerations all jostle for attention and belie the notion that this is a simple situation with easy solutions. The main part of this book will concern itself with some of the potential solutions to identifiable problems within the UK. It will deal with practical and achievable goals, and analyse in detail how we can learn from past mistakes. Nonetheless, it is a chastening thought that the big money is not being spent on the 'war on drugs'. The real war is not 'on' but 'for' drugs and the power that control of the drugs trade brings.

2

Just say 'I don't know': the challenge for education

A cornerstone of 'Tackling Drugs Together', the UK government's latest and most successful attempt to co-ordinate drugs policy across central and local government departments and agencies, is 'demand reduction'. While continuing with enforcement and treatment initiatives, the government has accepted, quite logically and in the face of overwhelming evidence, that the 'drugs problem' will never be eradicated by police and customs alone. There also seems to be an acceptance that 'grower' countries will never be able, or in some cases willing, to stop drugs production; that while there is a demand, there will always be a supply.

Demand reduction can take many forms, from increasing the emphasis of policing on arresting users, and thus making the potential consequence of drug use much less desirable, to 'educating' young people in order that they don't take drugs.

A third alternative is workplace drug testing. Already in use for jobs such as train driving, workplace drug testing is intrusive and liable to produce mistakes and unfair dismissals – what about people being 'set up', or slipped drugs unwantedly, or simply eating hash cakes by mistake at parties?

Of these policy options, arresting users would be much the most palatable to the right wing and to the press, but it didn't work in the 1960s and 1970s when the problem was on a much smaller scale, and there is no reason to suspect it would work now. Locking away large numbers of drug users, especially users of drugs such as cannabis, would swamp the prison system and, bearing in mind how easy it is to get drugs in prison, would not deter, only encourage.

Education

In reality, it is on drugs education that the success or failure of demand reduction rests. Three ministries, Education, Health and the Home Office, now fund drugs education initiatives.

The problem for educators is: how on earth do you 'educate' young people into not taking drugs? Over the years a number of different approaches to drugs education have been attempted, and if persuading young people not to take drugs has been the aim, they have so far failed miserably. Although attempts are currently being made to argue that 'Just Say No' has not necessarily failed, all the evidence points the other way. All the surveys, such as Parker and Measham's at Manchester University, are showing huge increases in teenage drug use. Since 1990 there has been an explosion of cannabis use by schoolchildren, and ecstasy use has already dramatically increased. The best gauge of levels of drug use and availability is street prices, which have either remained constant or fallen since 1987, against inflation. This is hardly surprising given that so much of what has gone on in the name of education has had no clear idea of how to achieve its goal, no understandable philosophy and no substantial time or resources allocated to schools and others engaged in the work. And it has always had as much of an eye on its public relations value – or at least its acceptability – as on its outcome.

Parker and Measham's research was showing by 1994 that 41 per cent of 15–16-year-olds had tried cannabis, 25 per cent had taken LSD, 22 per cent amyl nitrate, 16 per cent amphetamines, 13 per cent solvents, 12 per cent magic mushrooms, 7 per cent ecstasy, 5 per cent tranquillizers, 4 per cent cocaine and 3 per cent heroin. While Asians had tried less, black and white schoolchildren fared about the same, as did boys and girls, with the middle class only slightly behind the working classes. Furthermore, their work shows a year-on-year increase. By 1995 the overall number of triers had increased from 46 to 50 per cent.

Constraints

If, as has been the case so far, schools are to be the focus for drugs education, then some basic constraints need to be taken into consideration. However, there has previously been little sign that this has been the case. First, can education alone ever produce mass behaviour change in a given direction? Even with repressive and propagandistic educational systems, such as that of the old Soviet Union, for all those who became young Communist Party members, many more remained unimpressed, or rather preferred to believe the lessons learned in the school of harsh realities. Old nationalisms, old faiths and old greed withstood an intensive educational onslaught. What price, then, six hours of drugs education as part of an uncertified school health education programme, when compared to the realities, pressures and dreams of youth subculture?

The second basic problem that schools face is that of maintaining a positive public image while dealing with an emotive and therefore controversial issue. Not only do you have to educate, but you have to be seen to be giving messages whose content and method of delivery are acceptable to the 'silent majority', or more likely the tabloid-minded media. The very fact of running a drugs education programme at all when the school down the road doesn't do so could be interpreted as your school responding to a 'drugs problem' within its walls – a positive initiative gets represented negatively. This problem became compounded when Local Management of Schools was introduced and educational establishments all had to start competing for pupils and funds. The very definite guidance given to all schools by the Department for Education and Employment as part of 'Tackling Drugs Together' – all schools are encouraged to have a working policy on drugs – goes some way towards overcoming this problem, in the sense that all schools should now have drugs on the agenda.

Unfortunately, the education department circular 4/95 is only guidance, not law. Schools are not obliged legally to provide drugs education. However, inspectors from Ofsted (Office for Standards in Education) will include drugs education in all future inspections, so the clout behind the new guidelines is pretty strong. The recommendations for action are not prescriptive either, still allowing schools considerable latitude in the educational approach they adopt towards drugs. The problem now is the temptation for schools to be 'seen' doing something that parents will like: in other words, the populist approach becomes very attractive, regardless of whether it works.

Repeating old failures

One noticeable effect of the latest initiative has been the re-emergence on a larger scale of drugs education approaches which have been tried and tested, and which failed, long ago. If we look at these, with one eye on their public relations value, then we can understand why they are so attractive to formal institutions.

A particularly popular method of drugs education down the years, which has come back strongly in recent times, is the 'shock/horror' approach. This is fuelled every so often by a sensational media story about a young person dying – usually a young person who can be represented unambiguously as a 'victim'; middle class, respectable family, first time they tried a drug, etc.

'Shock/horror' has many attractions. The philosophy behind it is clear: adults know that drug use is dangerous, wrong and must be stopped; young people would not take drugs if they knew just how dangerous drugs were; and therefore what is necessary is a graphic warning of the dangers. The way forward is therefore to use materials or individuals which/who show the most devastating and frightening effects of drugs possible. The 'Leah Betts' video, sent to all secondary schools, is an example of this approach. There is no doubting its impact on viewers. Classrooms full of crying young people are not uncommon when they watch this video. It undoubtedly upsets young people because it works on the emotions, but does it deter drug use, make drug users safer or help them deal with the problems of living in a culture where drugs are commonplace?

While this approach would appear to have much common sense about it, it has never worked. Studies like that of DeHaes in *Health*

Education Research (December 1987) have shown that, perversely, young people were more likely to experiment illegally with drugs after having had such 'education'! This is not surprising given that the model, on closer inspection, is oozing with flaws.

The immortality of youth

Let's take the basic premise that death is the overriding terror of drug use. Basically it doesn't stand up. If death were the deterrent this model requires it to be, then we would have wiped out smoking and drink-driving decades ago. When people decide to use substances, fear of adverse effects is only one, usually relatively small, factor in that decision. With teenagers it is an even smaller factor. Teenagers all know that they are immortal, that it is other people who die; in any case, the risk itself adds to the attractiveness of the behaviour – adrenaline enhances the buzz, being someone who takes those risks marks you out above the conformist crowd. Those who go hang-gliding or mountain climbing know they could die. They assess the risks, take all possible precautions and then go ahead. We don't try to scare them out of pursuing their hobbies because we don't believe we have the right and because we know it would be pointless. If there were no danger, they wouldn't be doing it.

Besides all this, hundreds of thousands of people are seen to be dying from the use of *legal* substances, whereas only a few hundred deaths each year are attributed to illegal drug use. Young people's experience of drug use by those around them is generally that those people have a brilliant time. The desire to have a slice of that brilliant time is a much bigger factor than fear of death. We have worked at our agency with groups of young people who have been hospitalized and nearly died from the use of ecstasy, only to return a week later and take more pills.

When the press announced, in the Leah Betts case, that she had not died of an impure 'E', as was at first suggested, and that, on the contrary, the 'apple E' she took was pure MDMA (the active ingredient in ecstasy), there was a sudden increase in demand for 'apples'. Leah was regarded as 'unlucky' or not knowing what she was doing – drinking too much water while not dancing – and clearly with so much fake or adulterated 'E' around, here was a chance of guaranteeing the real McCoy. The messages we think we send are not necessarily those that are received.

Many of the early 'shock/horror' educational roadshows of the late 1970s and early 1980s featured needles and abscesses, gangrene and overdose. This illustrates another reason why the approach didn't work. In most parts of the country heroin use is very much a minority sport for young people. They don't like heroin and they don't like needles in any case; the drug represents an image they don't like (about which more in the next chapter). Needle use usually occurs well into a drug-taking 'career' for the tiny minority who do it. For that small group, the images miss their target: while most of us recoil in horror at the sight of needles going into arms, those most likely to use them, or those already using them, don't have the same negative reaction. Indeed, for many heroin users, giving up the ritual of injecting is an important factor in giving up the substance.

So the fundamental problem is that the pictures and images presented by 'straight' adults to young people in an attempt to deter them only serve to illustrate their own lack of understanding and stereotyping of the world of drugs and drug use. The imagery and messages miss the mark and therefore become identified by the young for what they are: propaganda. The only thing worse in educational terms than propaganda is propaganda that is transparently poor.

What the 'shock/horror' approach does have, however, is good PR value. It is a popular approach with adults and parents in particular, because in commonsense terms it appears to be an unequivocal response. We can all feel good because we are doing something definite, something forceful. It is favoured because it works for us. If, as a school, you adopt this approach, you can present yourself as taking a 'strong line', as sending 'clear messages'.

If only it worked, all our problems would go away. But it doesn't. Educationalists knew by the mid-1980s that 'shock/horror' didn't hack it. The problem then was: what would work and would it be acceptable to schools? At the same time, drugs educational philosophy was increasingly coming into the hands of the 'liberal' thinkers. In 1986 the government made finance available to Local Education Authorities to appoint Drugs Education Co-ordinators (DECs) to develop a new anti-drug drive. Unfortunately for the government, many of those appointed didn't believe that drug taking was, in itself, the evil it had been painted. Many more didn't believe that preventing young people from using drugs was an achievable aim.

The 'initiation' conference for the DECs, at Southampton University in autumn 1986, despite attempts at stage management was largely dominated by organizations like the Teachers' Advisory Council on Alcohol and Drug Education (TACADE), which believed that tackling drugs centred around fostering self-esteem and decision-making skills in young people, who would then be able to make healthy choices and resist peer pressure. At the fringe of the conference, the Institute for the Study of Drug Dependence (ISDD) was already persuading some DECs that harm reduction was the way forward.

New orthodoxies

So by 1986 there were two or three theories of drugs education which became, either individually or in combination, the orthodoxy of the 'experts'.

The first of these was the 'substance-focused' approach. The idea here was to give young people accurate information about drugs. The young people would assimilate this neutral information and then apply the lessons learned rationally to their own lives: they would see that drug taking was a bad idea and decide not to do it. Educationalists could thus successfully remove themselves from the role of propagandists and preachers, and morally distance themselves from the interventionist role by 'objectifying' information.

Once again this was an approach that had in-built problems. One major difficulty is that it was basically dishonest. The hidden agenda, and one that isn't even hidden in school reality, is still to stop people using drugs illegally. While many people would agree with the aim, it actually compromises the method. Once again evaluations, like that of DeHaes cited earlier, showed the approach to have no effect on young people's behaviour, and it is not difficult to see why. Information is not neutral in reality. If we hope to discourage young people from using illegal drugs by giving them accurate information, then the fact that the legal and socially acceptable substances like alcohol are at least as, if not more, dangerous than many illegal ones is hardly going to have deterrent value *per se*. To give such information may be honest, but it will hardly alone be sufficient to achieve the aim for drugs education perceived by wider society – to stop or at least discourage illegal drug use.

More nonsensical still is the fact that much of the basic information being given out was itself not free from bias. If you look at the drugs education literature and resources used in the mid to late 1980s, you will hardly see a bad word spoken about cannabis. Its effect on the lungs barely warrants a mention, and it is the nicotine in 'spliffs' that is seen as the major danger. As we show elsewhere, information about cannabis is never free from value judgement. The drug represents or symbolizes a focus of the 1960s battle of social values from which it never escaped: freedom of individual behaviour against the suffocating restraints of traditional moral codes; the counter-culture against the establishment. As a result, the information is selectively viewed and given in support of one or other of two extreme positions. The drug becomes 'good' or 'bad', and information that doesn't fit the image is not included.

The price we paid for this approach to information giving about cannabis was a generation who grew up proudly informing the world that cannabis was 'safer than alcohol' and 'not addictive', regardless of research, fact or even, dare I say, common sense. The reader will understand what I mean because the chances are that you will already have formed a judgement as to my own views and political persuasion based on the little I have said about the drug.

Given this basic lack of neutrality of information, and therefore the fact that the whole premise of the 'substance-focused' approach is false, the choice for educators becomes one of which information to give. In order to make that choice, the decision has to be made as to what the aims of drugs education really are. We are not neutral; we cannot remove ourselves from responsibility for our interventions. The debate in the late 1980s became focused on important central questions. Should we argue for abstention from the use of all drugs, legal and illegal, on health grounds? Should we play the socially acceptable game of pretending that certain drugs are more or less dangerous than they really are, in order to stay safely within existing mythologies? What were we trying to do?

The additional problem for the model was that information alone doesn't change behaviour in any case. Drugs are not used in a void; they are used in complex social situations by individuals buffeted by conflicting influences and pressures from without and from within. And in any case, how much factual information will young people be able to recall when they are offered a drug maybe years after a drugs education lesson? Are there key facts to be emphasized in the hope that they will be retained? Or are we trying to create, through the use of information, an overall impression or lasting image of drugs which will be influential at key stages later in life? We should have made a major effort to answer at least a few of these questions, but the debate never took place.

Perhaps the most important question the field needed to ask at the time is: was Marshall McLuhan right? Is the medium the message? It should have been clear that, given increasing drug usage by young people, the information about risks was not being believed, but few bothered to ask why. Newham Drugs Advice Project (NDAP) together with the Newham Education Authority did so, and the answer was that who gave the information was at least as important as the information itself. This topic will form the central discussion of Chapter 3. At the time, nobody listened to what we had to say.

Another, and greater, orthodoxy of the time was that of the 'person-focused' approach. As the title implies, this placed the emphasis on the individual rather than the drug, and on personal skills rather than on information. In fact, information was of such low status in this method that I can recall being told by one proponent of the theory that drugs information was irrelevant so long as the skills and self-esteem existed.

The whole notion of the 'person-focused' approach came from the USA, where the emphasis was placed on the autonomy of the individual and the freedom to choose. The idea was that young people needed help in their self-development to the point where, while remaining free to choose, they would have the skills and self-esteem to resist pressure from others to take drugs. This means helping young people explore their own attitudes, improve their decision-making skills, and increase their social skills in order to resist peer group pressure.

Once again the basic assumption is that any sane and strong individual would not take drugs. Those who do so, therefore, are irrational or weak. They are surrounded by the negative influences of peers (a kind of cold war mentally where you can trust nobody) and need help to avoid becoming drug-using sheep. This is a dangerously adult view of the world of young people. When we were young the world didn't seem that way. It is based on an adult distrust of young people. At its most extreme, this model results in rows of 10-year-olds in the classroom having their social skills and freedoms enhanced by practising different ways of saying 'no' to each other (there are eight different ways apparently).

The fact that the peer group and peer pressure rarely operate in this way (the term 'peer group temptation' seems much more appropriate – see Chapter 3) and are not always negative, and that such rehearsals have no effect on behaviour in the outside world, doesn't seem to prevent this model from being adopted again and again in different forms. Two favoured versions at the moment are the 'DARE' programme, running mainly in Nottinghamshire schools and supported by the local police, and 'Project Charlie', which operates in Tower Hamlets among other places. 'Life Education Centres', an Australian operation imported to the UK, runs a similar programme from high-tech touring buses. Once again, whether it works in reality is less important than the public relations value of having kids go through it; those 10-year-olds look good on TV. We adults can feel reassured that something definite is being done.

However, there is a bigger problem with this model. A model based on the individualistic freedom to choose, the 'anyone can be anything if they dream and work hard enough for it', Wizard-of-Oz view of the world, is actually dangerous to the well-being of young people. Yes, we all have decisions to make, but in reality those decisions are never really free. The pressures on the individual to make certain choices are always more heavily weighted in one direction than another. People exist in socioeconomic realities; for some young people, choices and opportunities are severely limited, alternatives few and expensive. In its biggest sense, pretending that people are 'free to choose' is a political lie.

While not denying individual responsibility for action, the danger of pretending that this is all that is going on, is that the individual drug user becomes seen as someone acting out of perversity rather than in response to a set of personal and social circumstances. We can say to the individual whose 'free' choice was actually to use drugs: 'We gave you the skills, we fostered your self-esteem and you still made the wrong decision. It's your own fault.' Let's not fool ourselves about 'freedom to choose'; there is a right choice (maybe substitute 'healthy' or 'legal' as professional-speak for 'right') and a wrong choice (illegal drugs, as Michael Howard so clearly defined it on the 'Tackling Drugs Together' anniversary).

Of course, if it's the individual's fault, society has little or no responsibility for helping with their drug problems. The individual has made a wrong choice and must therefore suffer the consequences. You feel much less inclined to offer support to those you have warned and who have rejected your advice. In the late 1980s, ISDD warned that this approach could lead to 'victim blaming'; it certainly led easily to blaming young people, although the word 'victim' once again suggests an inaccurate interpretation of drug use. Drug users may develop problems which need our support, but that does not make them 'victims'. Interestingly, in Britain if you were under 16 years of age in the late 1980s (and in most places right up to the present day), your chances of getting help with a drug problem were virtually nil because the services did not exist. You had to wait until you were an 18-year-old heroin user before services were interested in you.

There is also a problem for 'person-focused' approaches in educational practice: what are decision-making skills and how do you teach them? To teach skills, they need to be identified, broken down into component parts and then practised in a planned programme with structured progression; then they need to be practised in the real world. Schools are usually very bad places to be doing this. In day-to-day schooling, young people get few chances to make decisions – about their education, their dress, their language, their behaviour – but plenty of opportunity to learn about doing what you're told.

This is not surprising because it is an important part of what schools are about. They are institutions of social control designed to fit people into a society in which they will also have only limited choices about what will affect the circumstances of their lives – whether there are jobs available, whether they will be made redundant, what leisure facilities will be available to them, what the mortgage rate will be.

I don't wish to imply that individuals have no responsibility for their actions, that they are sent hither and thither with no control over their lives. Rather, I am arguing that in order for people to face up to their responsibilities and shape their own destinies to a greater extent, we need something way beyond one classroom hour a week where you get a chance to express an opinion.

This role for schools in shaping young people to conform with the needs of society impacts directly upon the effectiveness of drugs education. Schools must have order and must protect the interests of the majority, and they must be seen to do so by parents and public. This can lead to a conflict between the pastoral ethos of many schools and classroom practice. It is no good expecting open and honest class discussion about drugs and our attitudes towards them in class if the school calls in the police the moment a young person is found with a joint. Try doing some in-service training on drugs with professionals and you'll soon see just how limited an 'open and honest' discussion becomes. This is, after all, illegal behaviour we're talking about. And being identified has consequences. Thankfully, one of the better aspects of recent guidance from the Department for Education and Employment is the emphasis on graded responses to individual drug use, which must include care and support for the individual.

Another positive suggestion from the education department is for cross-curricular work which looks at drug use in a broader context than that of individual behaviour. Drugs have a history, a politics, an economy, a biology, a chemistry and so on. Only by really educating, rather than by simple behaviourist practice, can we begin as a society to understand and get to grips with the issue of drugs. It always used to amaze me that during discussions young people could say that smoking cannabis at home alone didn't affect anybody else, and that therefore it was up to the individual alone whether they smoked it. Cannabis use was described as 'the victimless crime' and 'not hurting anyone'. Yet what was being described was the smoking of a substance which had come halfway around the globe affecting the lives of peasant farmers thousands of miles away, and hence through many money-making, grubby hands.

The 'no damage' view is the inevitable consequence of educating for a world in which the individual is all important and self-defining.

The need for a new impetus

If all these approaches to drugs education failed, by the early 1990s the argument among educationalists was shifting once again. If you couldn't stop them doing it, some argued, then you should educate them to reduce the harm they are coming to. Let's teach them about using drugs less dangerously. It is an approach which had been adopted by health education in response to HIV/AIDS, and which influential figures in the drugs field, such as Nicholas Dorn of ISDD, had long been arguing applied equally to drugs.

The problem in the classroom was how to give such information to groups, only some members of which would already have tried drugs, without appearing to say to everyone 'you can take drugs with little risk of any consequences'. We were by now at the opposite end of the spectrum from 'shock/horror' and that included public relations value. This approach offered adults and schools no clear and simple answers. It appeared to accept drug use and say, 'well it's going to go on, we can only take rearguard action'. I remember being told by a school inspector that harm reduction would never be taught in the classroom because it was so controversial and could encourage drug use by previous non-users.

Indeed, the whole theory, while long since accepted by the drugs field as an orthodoxy, is still considered so controversial that it is not mentioned in 'Tackling Drugs Together'. Instead there is a new language which allows elements of harm reduction to occur while accepting no real responsibility for the fact. Since the Home Office introduced the Drugs Prevention Initiative at the beginning of the decade and then had to decide whether prevention meant abstention, and whether its success in achieving abstention was what it wanted to be evaluated upon, we have had the language of primary and secondary prevention: in the first place, we don't want people to take drugs, but in the second place, if they do take them, we don't want them to come to any harm.

Harm reduction does, however, give us clear and potentially more achievable aims. Dorn argues that most experimenters with drugs in most social groups already have their own informal procedures for the reduction of harmful consequences, and that we should aim to build upon these. This acknowledges that peer groups can be a positive influence, but demands that we understand how they operate – their belief systems and behaviour patterns. This involves the kind of listening to and valuing of young people's experience to which the person-focused approach has at least opened the door.

However, ultimately harm reduction is saying, 'we can't stop them doing it'. Howard Parker argues exactly that point: young people will experiment and use drugs recreationally no matter what we do. Accusations of defeatism seem entirely justified here. We are not powerless, as I shall explain later. To say we can have no effect is to argue that no public health educational initiatives work. The evidence, from personal hygiene to immunization to personal fitness regimes, is that we can actually do a lot – but not if we do it badly, and if we aren't even sure what we're trying to do.

In this chapter, we have looked at the history and dilemmas of drugs education in the formal educational system. It is not a history of success, but it makes us face up to some of the most important questions involved in drugs education. If all the messages have failed or are too controversial to touch, are we using the right messenger? If schools have to face major constraints in delivering drugs education, are there other places and other media through which this education might take place? Are prevention and harm reduction incompatible concepts? Is it possible to prevent or deter young people from experimenting with drugs? What is the relationship between education and pastoral care? What do young people themselves think about drugs education and drugs services?

By 1991 these were questions that a number of us working in the field were asking ourselves. In the next three chapters I will attempt to look at some positive answers.

3

The real 'secret society'

Just what is going on out there?

The main problem for drugs education is the same problem as that faced by mainstream drug treatment services in trying to access the young: we haven't got a clue what they're doing. We don't know what the experience of the young now is like because as adults we, the policy and decision makers, the professionals, are too far removed from it. The generation gap has become a generation gulf.

In tribal societies, the old were revered and respected. They carried with them information which was of practical use in terms of survival; they knew from experience where food would be, which berries were safe, how to skin a wild animal. All the information a young person needed in life was gained from adults whom he or she knew, so they were listened to. And along with the practical came the moral and spiritual guidance. The whole community had a unity of spirit and purpose then. This has all gone. Spiritually, in the modern western world, even the established church is regarded by some as an 'add-on', a luxury in life, and by others as something the 'cranks' believe in. In a godless society, a relative universe, there is no absolute right or wrong: they are subjective concepts, open to question.

What is more, people of my generation, born in the age of steam trains, one-channel TV, pre-computer, pre-space race and with the prospect of a 'secure job for life', have little useful advice or information we can hand down. We can only love our young and hope they find a way through life. They know more about how the world they live in operates than we do: our education did not cover the quantum theory or RAM or soft logic; we did not watch endless acts of violence on TV or have sex thrust at us from the pages of every magazine; we did not have to face large-scale unemployment surrounded by fabulous material wealth. We didn't have HIV: we'd only just got the pill in our teenage years. The world changes so fast that each new generation just shrugs off the last, having less and less in common with it and valuing it even less. Our old people aren't revered, they're irrelevant. We don't give them pride of place – we put them in nursing homes and sell their houses to pay for it.

Add to this gap the traditionally closed doors of youth subculture. It is designed to keep us out. That is why it has its own language, gestures, clothes, music, imagery, ideas and values. They are not meant to be shared with adults. As soon as adults try to keep up – and they do try because the pressure in our society is to look young, that's what fashion dictates – the whole scene changes. Nobody wants their party gatecrashed by the oldest swinger in town. It's embarrassing! We can remember that feeling ourselves.

So how do we engage with it? If we aren't allowed in, how do we find out what's going on? I don't mean how many are taking which drug at what age. I mean what do they think, these young people, about the drugs scene as part of the world they live in? And when we've found out what they think, how do we communicate with them about it on a real and meaningful level, on a level that will change anything?

Many would argue that we have no right to change the world of young people at all, but I cannot agree. The experience I do have as an adult is of the world as a problematic place where mistakes can have far-reaching consequences. I do have a role to play in helping them learn because I know the nonsense I got told about sex and drugs when I was young, and street bullshit, in essence, never changes.

It's not like that in real life

The mistake is to believe that nothing else has changed in anything but outward form, and to think that we can blunder in dishing out the advice. It might make us feel good, but they're not listening. We can make some terrible mistakes and end up presenting to young people a version of the world they live in which has nothing in it that they can recognize.

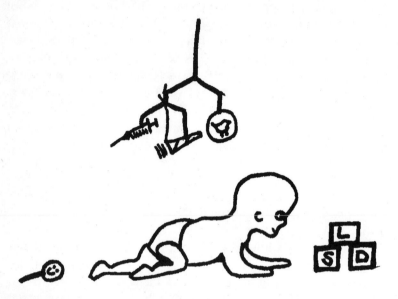

Peer pressure – or growing up in a world of drugs

A prime example of this in drugs education is the old favourite, peer pressure. In the late 1980s, schools in the UK were circulated with a drugs education video called *Minder, a little bit of give and take*, starring George Cole and Dennis Waterman in the TV personas. In this video a lad who has never taken drugs, and has no reason to think his friends have either, is suddenly confronted with his mates trying to get him to take heroin. He's told he's a softy for not having a go and is ostracized socially. This is rubbish. This is not how it happens. Where did we get the idea from?

The chances are that in the real world you'll know some friends who have tried cannabis. You'll watch them smoke it, see them giggling over nothing, listen to them say how much fun it is, find it funny when they crave for endless sweets or forget what they're saying in mid-sentence. It'll get passed to you and sooner or later you'll have a go. Any pressure is likely to be a mild tease (I'm not saying always, just usually). What is going on is more peer temptation than peer pressure. It looks good, you want to try it. You want to be part of the group fun. You want in. You will probably feel nervous and excited about it at first, but soon it just becomes a normal group activity, something that bonds the group together. Where is the victim here? Where is the pressure? Inside the self.

The concept of peer pressure is based on the false concepts of the 'war on drugs', where our young, in order not to be the enemy, must be victims. They are good really, so they must have been forced into being bad by those 'bad influences' around them. The trouble with thinking this way is that it allows young people to abdicate all responsibility for their own decisions. Young people choose to take drugs; they don't have to. They usually want to. They're curious, they're tempted, they try it, they enjoy it (it wasn't as scary as they thought it would be – a bit of a laugh really) and they take it again. Certainly there is a desire to conform in operation here, but it is internal, not external.

I am reminded of the tale told by Alysoun Moon and Noreen Whetton about the 'Jugs and Herrings' draw-and-write research technique into primary schoolchildren's attitudes to and knowledge of drugs, which informed their 'Health for Life' books. The technique involves getting children to draw and write their responses to a scenario and questions concerning a drugs scene in which a child finds a bag of drugs on the path on the way home from school. When asked what he would do with the bag, one boy wrote that he would 'find someone to persuade me to take them'. Even primary schoolchildren are aware of how the concept of peer pressure can absolve them of responsibility.

Young people need to learn to take on responsibility, and in my experience they respond extremely well to being given it, provided it is done in the right way. There is a danger that we see all young people as the evil pressures or the good but helpless victims. I work with young people every day and have done for nearly twenty years, and this is not my experience of them. In my experience they respond as sensibly as adults to a given situation, bearing in mind that they come to it from a different perspective. In the main they're not evil, they're not weak, they're not stupid, they're just young. (There are, of course, exceptions to any generalization, but they do not make the rule.)

Alien nation

We are in danger of viewing our young as such a problem that we will burn all bridges with them. Communicating across a widening gap is getting harder, but it is far from impossible. If we don't find effective ways of doing it, where we can help them to deal with the problems they face without looking down on them or judging them all the time, then we'll be in big trouble as a society.

The demonstration of youth is not new. An excellent book by Stanley Cohen, *Folkdevils and Moral Panics*, charts the history of the phenomenon much better than I can do here. What is clear is that the more the adult establishment rails against a youth culture, the stronger it makes it. When rock stars were getting arrested for drugs in the 1960s, when 'long-haired weirdo' hippies were the outrage on the front pages of the tabloids, the young felt proud to be part of the 'love generation'. When the furore died down and the marketing men began selling love beads, the whole thing died away. Each youth subculture has to have things it stands against possibly more than those it stands for: hippydom had the Vietnam War and adult outrage to solidify it, to give it its identity. Without reference to things outside yourself, your identity dissipates. You could argue equally that the increasing hysteria and clampdowns on rave culture in the UK have given a hedonistic movement something to rail against – the Criminal Justice Act – and so prolonged its life by five years. Equally, the endless warnings against ecstasy at raves were, in the early days, guaranteed to attract drug dealers to a new market and to get young people rallying around a new cause.

Instead of working against youth culture, we need to work with it, to become part of it, to enable it to deliver the messages we think are important in ways which it can live with, and which will have effect because they are the ways all the rest of their information is transmitted between young people.

I was reminded of this approach in 1990 when, becoming increasingly disillusioned with the effectiveness of drugs education and drugs services for young people, I chanced one day on an old copy of *Oz* magazine my mother had kept in a bundle of my old possessions. Reading it, I was struck by a number of key ideas. First, it had some intelligent and high-quality drugs information, some of it harm reduction about LSD, some of it directly judgmental of amphetamines – the 'Speed Kills' slogan was a hippy thing. Second, the artwork was brilliant – it drew the eye to the page and made you want to possess it and read it. Third, it has attitude: it stood squarely for the values of young people because it was written by young people for young people. The language was right, the ideas were right; I identified with it all again, immediately across the gulf of time. Powerful stuff! If we could only recreate drugs education and drugs services in that way. 'Release' was, after all, the first drugs service set up by the young for the young, way back in the 1960s. We seemed to have forgotten the lesson.

Bridging the gap

In order to bridge the gap, we needed intermediaries, those scouts who could tell us what was happening out there. In 1990, NDAP and Newham Education Authority undertook some 'research' into young people and drugs. There was no intention to publish. We just wanted an open dialogue so that we could find out what problems young people had with drugs, what they thought of drugs education and why they weren't using drugs services. We didn't have any money, so we enlisted research degree students from what is now the University of East London. Each had a slightly different angle because each wanted the work to go towards their degree, but the two main techniques used were recorded or noted conversations and sealed, confidential questionnaires. Additionally, NDAP staff and

and myself watched young people in drama classes in local schools improvising going for help with a drug problem.

When we sat down to piece together the results and impressions, we were faced with the realization that we had to go back to the drawing board.

Of drugs education, young people said that they believed very little. They felt that teachers and other adults had a judgmental attitude which extended beyond drugs to embrace much of youth culture, and this made much of what they said 'suspect'. The messenger was as important as the message in terms of the credibility of the information. What is more, credibility rested not just on who was delivering the message, but on the style of delivery. A Home Office evaluation of our approach has confirmed this point. A 'relaxed' method of communication was important; there had to be no element of 'preaching'.

Adults generally suffered from being perceived as not knowing what they were talking about, or being embarrassingly out of touch. Young people thought that they often knew more about drugs than those who were teaching them. We have found through our work since then that young people will ask questions designed to establish teachers' knowledge of the subject before they will be listened to: 'What's a "cally" and is it the same as a "purple ohm"? What have you got to tell me then? If you don't know about the drugs and can't understand my world, then what can you teach me?'

Interestingly, in the credibility stakes, people the same age as themselves were also not rated highly in terms of information deliveries. They didn't trust their peers not to bullshit; they didn't believe they knew any more than the recipients themselves, and they didn't want them to either because this would confer an 'élite' or 'superior' status on a special few which was resented. Peer education is not an instant panacea; it has be properly thought through.

The credible individual was seen as slightly older, say 18–25 years. These young adults were seen as 'walking the walk, talking the talk'. They led the lifestyle that the 14–16-year-old aspired to: they were mobile, went to clubs, had been there, seen it, done it. They were seen as independent and experienced of drugs, particularly the drugs familiar to their own environment. Any old ex drug user would not do. Placing an ex heroin user in front of people who were surrounded by a cannabis and ecstasy scene would achieve nothing. There had to be an identification, a feeling that the information givers knew what it was like to be part of that scene at that age, even though they had left it behind.

The classroom resources were seen as unattractive and unglamorous. Photocopied A4 worksheets didn't make the grade. This generation got its information from glossy magazines aimed specifically at them. The quality of the resources in presentational and image terms indicated how much the young people were valued and respected. The language and sentence structure of many classroom resources were felt to be too hard to understand.

Additionally, too often the 'right' or 'required' responses to questions in class exercises or discussions were seen to be obvious, telegraphed. 'If someone offered you this drug at a party, what would you do?' 'Say I don't want it.' No thought, no learning. Happy adult, untouched young person. Give any other response and you got 'nagged at'. This all added to the feeling of being on the end of a propaganda exercise.

Drugs services didn't fare any better. Young people thought they were places where 'junkies' went, 'junkies' being 'old' heroin users with whom they had nothing in common. If the place catered for 'junkies', what did it have to offer them? In the East End of London, most teenagers did not approve of heroin, injecting or the lowlife image that went with either. 'Their' drugs were cannabis, stimulants and hallucinogens. The problems they faced were not where to get supplies of clean needles. Young people identified an entirely different set of problems. They were concerned about drug debts, especially since it was easy to run debt: local dealers would often allow you to buy more than you could afford and then pay later. This often ended in threats, violence or stealing.

Young people also often felt trapped into a drug-using lifestyle where everyone they knew took drugs, talked about drug experiences or went looking for drugs. This taking over of their lives often concerned them because breaking out was hard. 'If you go round a mate's house, they're smoking a draw. Go to a party and they're "E"ing it or "tripping". Hang round the street and there: nothing to do except get stoned. It's hard to even cut down.' Many felt out of control of their drug use as a result, although they didn't always want to give up, they just wanted to be in charge again.

They identified health problems as a concern, but not dying. They were concerned about their mental state as a result of using hallucinogens and stimulants; fear of 'losing it' emotionally or psychologically was quite common.

Others were using drugs, especially solvents, to blot out physical or sexual abuse or bullying. They commonly felt there was no one in a drugs agency who would understand or be able to help with either solvent use or abuse by adults.

Some were concerned at the problems their drug use was causing for relationships with friends or family. Others worried that their school work was suffering because they were 'out of it' for too much of the time. Some were worried by the violence around drugs, either their own or others' use of violence. Still more were worried about drug use by family members or about family dealing from the house.

Drugs services were not seen as catering for any of these problems. Young people felt too embarrassed to go to a drugs project with a problem around cannabis use, because they had been told it wasn't a problem drug and felt they would get laughed at or told they were imagining it. Drugs workers were seen as 'social workers', which meant that the minute you entered a project, these adults with power would start to take decisions for you. Things would no longer be in your control. They might even take you into care. Young people's experience of adults was of being talked 'at' or 'about' by them, not of being talked 'to'. They certainly found it hard to believe that adults would respect confidentiality. They had no experience of this. Their impression was that drugs workers would immediately contact parents, the school or other professionals, and they usually wished to avoid this at all costs.

The overall impression was that young people existed in a drastic power imbalance with adults, and that being under the influence of that power would lead them into unknown areas with potentially catastrophic results. In other words, help was seen not as help, but as disaster.

Even when these other problems were surmounted, young people said that services were inaccessible. They were too far away. Travelling out of their own area was seen by many as 'dangerous' because it meant crossing other groups' 'manors' (territory). Others simply hadn't got the money or the time to make several visits to a project without questions being asked at home which would blow their confidentiality. On top of this, services were open during office hours when they were meant to be at school.

If young people's drug use was already difficult to access because of the barriers of subculture and illegality, it was clear that the response of adult professionals was actually increasing that inaccessibility. In order for drugs education to be effective and for drugs services to access young people, there needed to be a major rethink. It is just that rethink that is proving controversial for the government, because it doesn't fit in with the media rhetoric of the 'war on drugs'.

Ways forward

The research points the way quite clearly to solutions to both the above problems, but those solutions need careful selling to a press looking to label someone 'soft on drugs'.

The basic requirement is to use properly trained adults with experience of the street drugs scene to deliver both education and treatment services. This service needs to create a profile, an image, for itself that is credible in the eyes of young people, and this involves marketing on a number of levels. Publicity for the service needs to involve young artists and designers, and both publicity and educational materials need to be of the highest quality, matching the best of the magazines, flyers and other paraphernalia which make up the youth market today. The information materials need to be scrupulously honest and impartial, need to be crafted by young people and need to be available in a variety of media. Young adults from the service need to take the education and the treatment packages out to where young people are: schools, youth centres, clubs, parks, McDonald's. The whole service, especially the counselling, requires person-centred, non-judgmental approaches with empowerment and acceptance of responsibility as key elements.

Large rave organizations market themselves through records, video, magazines, CD-ROM, flyers, T-shirts, badges, caps, jackets and other merchandise. They are credible with young people. Provided a drugs service does it correctly and doesn't come across as some evangelical 'Guardian Angels' type of organization, there is no reason why it should not do the same. Instead of some pale version of statutory services, a young people's drug project should be enterprising, independent and firmly part of the same subculture. As the old saying goes, 'why should the Devil have all the best tunes?'

In Chapter 5 we will look in detail at how this might be achieved. Certainly my own organization, NDAP, has gone a long way towards establishing this model in the form of its Youth Awareness Programme (YAP), and we can learn a lot from the process we have undertaken. Before we do this, however, let us 'flag up' some of the potential pitfalls.

Any such service must walk a tightrope. Fall to one side and you lose young people. Fall to the other and the establishment will hang you.

The good name of the school

To operate such a service as the one described above, the first hurdle to be overcome is gaining access to schools. From the point of view of public relations and parental satisfaction, headteachers are going to feel a lot happier about having the police or a health professional or just their own teachers delivering drugs education. This is undoubtedly storing up trouble if it means that little effective is being done in terms of student drug usage, but in the short term nobody can argue with respectable professionals coming into school.

Similarly, if drug use is identified, it would appear to be an easier and 'tougher' response to exclude those young people involved. However, the 'tough' option does not appear to be so advantageous to schools in practice. Expulsions for drugs attract publicity, and this is often contrary to the image of itself that the school wishes to portray. The impression is often raised in parents' minds that, if they're having to kick kids out for drugs, the school must have a drugs problem. You then have the worst of all worlds: the school gets a bad reputation, the young person receives no help for their drug use and the problem just gets shifted to another school or a pupil referral unit – the young person's education suffering in the process. What is more, such action has little or no effect on the drug use of other pupils, who merely get better at concealing what is going on. Classroom discussion of drugs becomes even more guarded, and even less is achieved.

The UK government did try to address this issue in the Department for Education and Employment circular 4/95, which states, in a major step forward, that 'schools will want to develop a repertoire of responses, incorporating both sanctions and counselling, reflecting the different kinds of drug-related offences, such as possession of an illegal drug, individual use and selling or sharing drugs with other pupils'. The circular continues:

> In cases where it is clear that a pupil is selling illegal drugs and the health and safety of other pupils is directly at risk, the headteacher may decide that a pupil should be excluded ... permanent exclusion may be warranted as a final sanction when all other reasonable steps have been taken ... In both [fixed and permanent exclusions] the school should take steps to ensure that the excluded pupil has access to professional support and advice from health and social services, including early intervention services. Schools should be aware of the range of specialised agencies, support and counselling services available in their areas which may be in a position to support an at risk pupil.

This pushing of schools away from pure punishment and towards an approach balancing discipline with support is to be commended, but it will take more than this to get schools responding to incidents pragmatically, flexibly and sensibly.

Other sections of the same document show that the need to be seen to be taking a strong line is still important: 'Although there is no statutory requirement to do so, the Secretary of State would expect the police to be informed when illegal drugs are found on a pupil or on school premises.'

Getting a balance is difficult because, as in the wider society, the mixture of law and order and health issues creates problems: the harder you police an issue, the further underground you drive it, making access for the health professionals more difficult. On the other hand, the more out in the open you get a problem, the bigger it seems to the public, and the more the law appears to be an ass; either a law is a law that we want and it is enforced, or it is a law we don't want and should be removed from the statute book. Similarly with schools, we can't have students openly smoking cannabis on the premises; this must be against school rules and those rules must be enforced if they are to be respected. There will, inevitably, be a cost in that young people will be careful about how they avoid conforming to these rules. So the real situation gets harder to access and more young people can get drawn into trouble.

We have found that one way of encouraging schools to ensure that the support systems operate effectively is for our counsellors to be on site in all schools in a locality at set times of the week, so that no school can be pointed to as having a particular problem. Access to counselling can therefore be pre-crisis and can be sold to parents as a positive intervention by the school in handling a social issue. This is strengthened by offering schools the same confidentiality that is offered to individuals. No statistical record is kept of numbers of referrals from particular schools; instead we use postal district. This way we avoid statistical data being used inappropriately to batter individual establishments. Numbers of referrals do not necessarily reflect the scale of problem: they can equally be a reflection of how safe young people feel in gaining access to support, of staff awareness and training, of an effective pastoral system and many other things.

The next main area of potential difficulty in working with young people below the age of adulthood is that of parental rights and responsibilities. While young people told us that lack of confidentiality was a major factor in their failing to access help, parents are also keen to know if their young person has a drug problem and whether they are receiving help. We are dealing with incompatible aims here. Parents want to be told. Young people don't want them to. Drugs workers feel an acute dilemma here. While telling some parents is potentially disastrous (we know of parents who have responded to their child's drug use by beating them so badly that they were hospitalized), the majority of parents clearly want to help and might feel angry that they were not given the opportunity to do so with their own child.

Many Local Education Authorities and schools have enshrined parental rights so strongly into their procedures that they confirm pupils' worst fears about the lack of confidentiality. Indeed, in circular 4/95 a draft policy for schools, written by the County Advisor for Drugs and Health Education in Cambridgeshire, Ruth Joyce, is reprinted as an example, presumably, of good practice: 'If a young person admits to using or supplying substances off the premises, the teacher's discretion will be involved, but informing the Substance Co-ordinator is appropriate action. The Co-ordinator should inform the headteacher, who will inform the parents.'

I'm not sure where the 'teacher's discretion' comes in here, as teachers' course of action is charted out. So if a young person, in a drugs education lesson, admits to smoking a spliff with friends (like the other 41 per cent in Parker and Measham's study), the parents are informed. No one will say anything in class. Even asking too knowledgeable a question might be regarded as suspect and drop you in deep trouble. If young people are continued to force to hide this issue, we cannot be surprised if they don't ask the questions they want and need answers to. If they operate in a world where they have no believable information about drugs, they'll be lost to street 'savvy', most of which is dangerously inaccurate. It is not in the interests of young people – or of parents – for young people to be frightened of finding information or going for help when they need it.

Resolving conflicting demands

How can this dilemma of conflicting demands be solved productively? Is there an answer in the framework of law which can see us through? Well, there is certainly a window of opportunity. Schools are under no legal obligation to inform parents, even if their child is involved in a drug-related incident. Schools therefore have a flexibility of response open to them, and they can enlist parental involvement when young people have been found to be using drugs in school – but this can be done in ways which will be more likely to encourage a productive outcome. Information gained about drug use outside school can be treated in a more considered fashion, depending on the nature and seriousness of the admission. By law, teachers cannot guarantee confidentiality, but they can, to quote circular 4/95, 'point to sources of confidential information and advice and to treatment and rehabilitation services to help those who are misusing illegal drugs to stop'.

But how confidential can this support be? The Children Act 1989 appears on the surface merely to restate the dilemma in its basic principles. These quotes, taken from *Issues of Substance* published by the National Children's Bureau, illustrate the point:

Children's wishes must be ascertained and taken into account in all dealings with them (depending on age and maturity) – even in emergency situations.

Everyone who has parental responsibility has to be informed about what is happening to the child and of any decisions made about him or her.

On the surface, this does not seem to offer much comfort to drugs counsellors, who know that, if they have to tell parents, the young people won't come at all. The constant fear at the back of the mind is of being sued by an irate parent for not telling them what was going on.

The closest to a court ruling on this that we have in the UK is the infamous Gillick case, relating to medical advice and treatment for minors given without parental knowledge or consent (contraceptive advice in the Gillick case). If we regard drugs counselling as medical advice, which is in itself arguable unless prescriptions or injecting equipment and advice are involved, then as Jane Goodsir of Release has stated: 'Strong parallels can be drawn between the harm-reduction objectives in AIDS and Drug Misuse Part 1 from the Advisory Council on the Misuse of Drugs and the guidance at issue in the Gillick case.' She goes on to say:

> In Gillick, the judges held that those honestly acting in the best interests of the girl would not be guilty of aiding and abetting a criminal offence – in this case, unlawful intercourse. But a doctor who instead intended to facilitate unlawful sex could be guilty of a criminal offence.

Drugs counsellors working with young people with drug problems would, obviously, be 'honestly acting in the best interests' of those young people by trying to help them to give up or to avoid coming to serious harm. The National Children's Bureau and Release both point out that, in order to comply with the Gillick ruling, drugs workers should establish:

- that the young person, although under 16 years of age, is of sufficient understanding and intelligence to understand the advice and be capable of making his or her own mind up on the matter in question;
- that they cannot persuade the young person to inform parents or to allow them to inform the parents that the young person is seeking drugs advice;
- that the young person is very likely to begin or to continue using drugs with or without drugs treatment;
- that unless the young person receives drugs advice or

> treatment the young person's physical or mental health or both are likely to suffer;
> - that the young person's best interests require the worker to give the young person drugs advice or treatment or both without parental consent.

There is no precedent in case law for parents being able to sue a health professional successfully for infringing their rights with regard to confidentiality. Provided that the aim of the worker is to protect the young person, the criminal law is not interested. The only grounds for suing the drugs worker would be for negligence. As long as the advice and information given was accurate and appropriate, there would be no grounds for arguing such a case. Indeed, it could be argued that if a young person approached a drugs worker for counselling, support, advice or information in confidence and if the worker either was not prepared to give it or was only prepared to do so in circumstances which would make that help unacceptable to the young person (by informing parents), there would be a better case for negligence.

In support of this case, there is no statutory duty for voluntary agencies to pass on confidential information to social services.

Legally, therefore, while the situation is far from clearly defined, providing a confidential drugs service for young people is entirely possible, and the clear implication of circular 4/95 is that it is desirable. It is preposterous that the situation has not been clarified, but to do so would lead us on to the battlefields of the war between the extreme right and the libertarian left. In the meantime, once again, young people lose because few drugs agencies have the courage even to work with under-16s, let along actively promote, market and take into public institutions a service specifically designed for them.

If you consider the fact that most drugs services and their workers spend most of their time playing down possible problems with the drugs that young people use, thus denying many young people the right to have a problem in the first place, for most young people the current situation is disastrous. It has taken the injection of a relatively small amount of money into the field of young people's work to make most agencies suddenly, and for the wrong reasons, start to take matters seriously.

The insanity of this situation is that the rewards for pressing ahead are so great. Since NDAP established a system of young, specially trained Youth Awareness Programme counsellors, working in schools in a confidential system, the number of young people gaining help with drug problems has gone through the roof. In Newham alone, the numbers receiving help went from single figures to over 150 per annum in the first two years of the service. Furthermore, now running the scheme in four London boroughs, we have had nothing but support from parents. The bottom line for most parents is this: 'I don't want my child to take drugs, but if they do I want them to stay alive, stay out of trouble, get help and get off them. I hope that my child will tell me if they do use drugs so that I can help them, but if them having to tell me means them not getting help, I'd prefer them to get help.'

The advantages of working with young people and not against them, and of establishing a service with a young image, involving and guided by young people, and operating on an outreach basis, extend beyond counselling to the education side. Old barriers are broken down.

What are we trying to do?

Ideas of prevention and harm reduction are presented as oppositional in the 'war on drugs' mentality, but this should not be the case. Truth is truth, information is power. The 1993 report by the Advisory Council on the Misuse of Drugs (ACMD), entitled *Drug Education in Schools: The need for a new impetus*, identified the following objectives of drugs education:

- to minimize the number of young people who ever engage in drug misuse;
- to delay the onset of first use for those who do not experiment at any time;

- to minimize the proportion of users who adopt particularly dangerous forms of misuse;
- to persuade those who are experimenting with or misusing drugs to stop;
- to enable any pupils who are misusing drugs or who have concerns about the misuse of drugs to seek help.

Doing it the YAP way

Until now, only the first two of these objectives have been attempted and, as was stated in the previous chapter, the attempts have failed. The service we established as a result of what young people told us has worked. Early in 1995 the Home Office Drugs Prevention Initiative published the results of fifteen months' evaluation of YAP's education programme: *Young People, Drugs and Peer Education: An evaluation of the Youth Awareness Programme*, by Michael Shiner and Tim Newburn. Allow me to quote from the report with reference of the ACMD objectives shown above:

> … there was a general feeling among respondents who had not used drugs that participation in the YAP workshop had reinforced their anti-drug views and their decision not to use drugs. For some this involved fairly major re-orientations of their attitudes to particular drugs.

> Turning to those respondents who had used drugs, there was some evidence that the information provided by YAP had an important role in terms of secondary prevention; that it had discouraged them from using other 'harder' drugs.

> Respondents' … accounts pointed to an increased awareness of harm reduction issues … They also indicated that this information was of practical use to them.

> … for people who have started to question their own use of drugs, peer interventions can have an important role in supporting and validating decisions to give up drugs or to cut down on existing levels of drug use. Given this pattern it is important that drug

education of the type developed by YAP is frequently available to young people so that appropriate information and advice is available to them at a time when they may, for whatever reason, be questioning their drug-related behaviour.

If the payoffs of refusing to get caught up in preaching at young people, of not using methods of drugs education that don't work, and of not playing the adult professional expertise card are so glaringly apparent, why isn't it happening everywhere? The UK government clearly now sees this as the way forward, as public pronouncements from ministers have shown. If this concept allows us to deliver stronger, and indeed more negative, information to young people about the drugs they use, while at the same time respecting them and their ability to decide for themselves, and if in doing so we clearly change behaviour, then why do both right and left pillory the initiative? The reason is obvious. People are playing politics with young people and their lives. This scheme attacks ideas central to both extremes, the paternalistic, moralistic, 'hang 'em and flog 'em' right and the 'legalize cannabis because it never did anybody any harm and it's people's right to use whatever they want' left.

In subsequent chapters we will look at how such a service can operate outside a school environment; at what it takes to make the service work efficiently and without exploitation; at what keeps it walking the tightrope; and at the ways in which such a service can bring together the initiatives of a number of government departments. Before we do this, however, we need to consider just what the information is that we are giving to young people, since it appears that information giving is a controversial area.

4

Wishful thinking: 'facts' as neutrals

The problems with facts

Facts are dangerous. If this were not the case, it would not be controversial for the UK government to suggest, as the drugs educationalists (including the police) have been saying for years, that young people need balanced information on which to base their decisions. Facts about drugs often offend people because they do not correspond to their strongly held attitudes towards drugs and drug users. Our attitudes are formed from accumulations of experiences, snippets or flashes of information, impressions left by headlines or film characters, personal experience of drugs, the drug use of those known to us, our own personalities and moralities, and a host of other influences. What they are rarely informed by is any appreciation of scientific evidence. The lack of proper research, and the 'contaminated' nature of some research because of its funding source, mean that such evidence is not plentiful.

Cannabis is the most commonly used drug among young people and, indeed, among all users of illegal drugs. In our experience it is the drug about which young people ask most, and yet it is the drug about which it is the hardest to gain unbiased factual information. Most people's first experience of illegal drug use involves smoking a 'spliff' with friends and, while some feel paranoid and sick as a result and never repeat the experience and others interpret no effect at all (enjoying cannabis is, to a certain extent, a 'learned' experience), most people have a lot of fun with it and wish to repeat the experience. During the initial process, they are usually told that it is non-addictive and safer than cigarettes and alcohol. This is 'street' information, but is it true?

Facts about cannabis are almost invariably used to support one side or the other of the debate about legalizing the drug. This results in partial or distorted information being presented as truth. The Legalize Cannabis Campaign and its splinters or related groups present evidence for the benign effects of the drug and argue that the biggest harm to cannabis users comes from society's responses to its use: exclusion from school; gaining a criminal record; being fined or imprisoned.

It is undoubtedly true that these responses can damage people's lives severely, but are they the greatest harm that we can come to from using the drug? It could also be argued that respect for the law itself is damaged by our current position. On the statute book the drug is illegal and yet vast numbers of people choose to ignore that law. The police say that they are little interested in users of cannabis and always err towards cautioning rather than charging, and yet more cannabis users end up in court than users of any other drug. What happens to you seems to depend on the policy of the police force in your part of the country, the mood of individual police officers, how much lip they're given during a stop and search, whether you're young or black, the attitude of the magistrate towards the drug or drug taking in general, and a host of other factors. One view might be that we ought to make up our minds. Either the drug is illegal and therefore punishable, or it should not be, in which case we should change the law.

The great pot debate

The debates about cannabis date back to the 1960s when it stood as a symbol of counter-culture freedoms, a badge of the fight against a stale, unthinking and repressive establishment. People took sides about it then and have stuck to them. The arguments became illogical. All heroin users used cannabis first, therefore cannabis leads to heroin use. It is a natural herb and is therefore safe.

We need to take a closer look at the drug, at the experience of it and at medical evidence for harm, before we form opinions.

Cannabis is a very interesting drug to experience because it has contrary effects simultaneously. This is because it is not an experience of one chemical. There are numerous 'cannabis', many of which have still not been isolated for testing individual effect.

Most interest centres on an ingredient called tetrahydro-cannabinol or THC, and the strength of cannabis is generally measured by THC content. THC has hallucinogenic properties and the mild hallucinogenic effects can be readily identified in the cannabis experience. Time becomes distorted and the world takes on a dream-like quality. Everyday sensory experience becomes intensified: listening to music, for example, is regarded as a more pleasurable experience that you can really 'get into' when stoned. The relative importance of different thoughts becomes difficult to assess: users often have conversations which they identify as significant or profound, but which to an outsider seem rambling or silly. There is an opening up of associations of ideas, images and emotions which can result in anything from bursts of creativity to fantasies to being unable to stop thinking that the person you're talking to is someone else. Paranoia also derives from the hallucinogenic side of cannabis.

But these mild hallucinogenic THC experiences are not the whole cannabis experience. Many of the other cannabinoids appear to have sedative properties which take the sensations of use in another direction. It is the sedative side that makes cannabis popular for relaxation. Often, being in a room full of cannabis smokers is like being with people who are so relaxed that they are glued to the armchairs, half-asleep. Red-eyed, tired-looking individuals debate for half an hour who is going to make the coffee; it is a lazy drug.

The combination of hallucinogen and sedative produces still further effects, often interpreted as amusing in social settings, although some may be problematic in the workplace or on the street. Inhibitions may be loosened and people become more sociable, talkative and prone to giggling over nothing that non-users would regard as funny. Reaction times, muscle control, manual dexterity and co-ordination are impaired, and simple tasks like actually

'I've figured out how to save the world. Now I've got to work out how to get out of this chair!'

making a cup of coffee without leaving kitchen surfaces covered in ingredients can become very difficult. Funny in the kitchen; not so funny in a car. Then there is short-term memory loss, forgetting where you put something a minute beforehand, forgetting what you are saying in mid-sentence.

Then there is the 'munchies': an uncontrollable desire for sweet foods in particular, or food in general. Although no one is sure what causes this, it seems likely that it is the result of a combination of the heightening of sensations caused by the THC and a desire for blood sugar and energy caused by the sedative effects. In any case, it is not satisfied by eating, no matter how much: the brain just doesn't seem to register the sugar intake and demands more.

This unique combination of effects makes the cannabis experience highly enjoyable for most users; indeed, even the irrational bouts of paranoia can be laughed at later. There is, of course, a downside to all this: if you can't co-ordinate or remember properly, and if you drift into a lazy dream world for much of the time, then you're not doing yourself any favours in the classroom or the workplace. In a car, you may have the accident at twenty miles an hour as opposed to fifty. These are not inconsiderable drawbacks.

The real areas for concern about cannabis lie in the effects of long-term chronic use (exactly those areas least likely to interest young people). Such effects are notoriously difficult to measure scientifically, as was the case with tobacco and alcohol. Conclusive proof of harm directly associated with the use of cannabis is hard to isolate because people lead complicated lifestyles involving the use of other substances, and because death certificates do not cite cannabis as a cause, merely the illness which may have resulted from it. But this should not lead to the extraordinary claims made by the pro-cannabis lobby that 'no one has ever died from taking cannabis', or that 'the only way you could die from taking cannabis is if someone dropped a 10 ton block of it on your head'. There is certainly now sufficient evidence to suggest otherwise.

To see why, we need to consider the method by which the vast majority of people use cannabis. For most people, eating hash cakes or drinking herbal cannabis tea is something reserved for special occasions; nearly all users smoke it. This makes it difficult to separate out the damage to health caused by cannabis smoke, smoke of any sort, and the smoke from the cigarette with which a 'spliff' is normally made. Cannabis smokers tend to mix their drug with the tobacco from a torn-open cigarette and smoke it in a hand-made cigarette with a rolled cardboard tube instead of a filter, thus allowing much more tar into the lungs. Cannabis is a heavily tar-laden substance, especially in its resinous form, known as 'hash' or 'resin' or 'solid'. Additionally, in order to gain maximum effect, cannabis smokers tend to hold the smoke in their lungs for much longer periods of time than cigarette smokers. Cannabis smoke also contains known mutagens and carcinogens. It is therefore logical to expect, and therefore to look for evidence, that smoking cannabis causes cancer and other respiratory problems.

The problem is that, as with cigarette smoking, there is likely to be a long latency of up to thirty years, which means that we will only be able to begin to identify significantly high correlations during the coming decade as the 1960s and 1970s generation of heavy long-term smokers begin to reach the end of that period. Epidemiological studies are, in any cases, made more difficult by the illegality of the practice in most countries, making human subjects hard to find. This has all led the pro-legalization lobby to argue either that there is no evidence of links with respiratory disease and cancer, or that it is the cigarette in the spliff or general smoking that causes the problem – a rather academic point, if it is still what people do with the drug that causes death.

There have, however, been reviews of both case study research and laboratory test-tube and animal research which point clearly in the direction of such harm. The Australian National Task Force on Cannabis and the World Health Organization have both carried out major reviews of evidence. These reviews point to a number of respiratory problems. Quoting their findings, the report of the Parliamentary Office of Science and Technology (POST), *Common Illegal Drugs and their Effects*, May 1996, stated:

> Clinical studies suggest that chronic cannabis smoking increases the prevalence of bronchitic symptoms and reduces respiratory function. Clinical and laboratory studies have shown changes in the lung tissue of chronic cannabis smokers that are believed to be precursors of carcinoma. Case reports suggest that cannabis smokers may run a higher risk of developing cancers of the aerodigestive tract.

These findings seem frighteningly similar to those which were coming out about tobacco use over thirty years ago. Given the large numbers of users of cannabis, we may well face the prospect that cannabis, far from being a 'soft' drug, will turn out to be the biggest killer of all the currently illegal substances. We need to ask ourselves the question: if this drug had just been produced by a pharmaceutical company and the above had been the results of the trials of that drug, would we give it a licence? This is not an argument for the continuation of existing legislation or support for incarcerating cannabis users; I am merely posing a question that needs answering. Certainly, all this information needs to be placed before young people before they make decisions about its use, rather than say – as a health promotion officer did on *Panorama* in 1995 – 'I am more concerned about the nicotine than I am about cannabis.'

There are other problems with cannabis, which we have seen repeatedly in our own casework experience, to do with mental health and dependence. The evidence of case studies around the world is that large doses of strong cannabis can produce a temporary psychotic state, usually lasting only for a few days, involving confused thoughts, amnesia, hallucinations and paranoid delusions. We have certainly worked with a number of users experiencing such problems. As most drugs agencies work almost exclusively with heroin or crack users and few see young people, this is largely a hidden problem, but it is very real. While there seem to be no long-term consequences, it can be an extremely unpleasant experience for those going through it.

This does not, in turn, lead to an acceptance of the diagnosis of 'cannabis psychosis' in those suffering longer-term psychotic symptoms like schizophrenia. There is little evidence for cannabis use precipitating latent psychosis. It is also quite common, in our experience, to find those with mental illness self-medicating with cannabis for its relaxant properties. Contrary to expectations, the drug can work against other medication, its hallucinogenic properties increasing paranoia and heightening symptoms of the illness, thus delaying recovery. The same applies to those who are 'coming off' hallucinogenic or stimulant drugs: cannabis use can delay recovery.

We have looked at the fun of using cannabis and at its safety in terms of health. We need also to deal with the non-addictive street myth, for that is what it is. In Chapter 1, I outlined a mechanism for drugs dependence which was based on revisiting pleasurable experience and so establishing habitual behaviour patterns that become hard to break. This model applies to behaviours such as gambling as well as to drug use. It is defined by a number of identifiable effects, all of which we have seen in cannabis users.

I must make it clear, however, before comparisons with heroin start coming out in counter-argument, that to say a drug can be addictive is not to say it will be or needs to be for everybody who takes it. We do not argue such a case for alcohol in order to prove that it can be dependence forming. Just as there is a world of difference between those who drink small amounts at social gatherings and the solitary problem drinker, so there is between the occasional 'spliff' smoker and the chronic user. We have worked with young people who are stoned all day, everyday, and who smoke over an ounce individually each week, but they are clearly the exception.

A feeling of compulsion to take a drug is the first measure of habit. We have worked with those who become anxious at the possibility of being without a smoke for just one evening, who are prepared to travel miles for a buy. Young people recognize this behaviour easily.

Another indicator is the regularity of pattern of use, smoking at the same time or the same place in a near-compulsive fashion. This is common experience to many cannabis users.

Drugs taking priority over other aspects of life is a third measure. Again, we know young people who would rather get stoned than go to school or to work, adults who would rather smoke than go out, and many who would rather spend their money, even money they haven't got, on cannabis rather than on bills.

The tendency to return to drug taking soon after a period of abstinence is another mark of dependence. There are now many thousands of old hippies in our society all saying they could stop 'smoking dope' at any time, but few doing so for more than a few days at a time. It certainly seems to be a drug that carries a strong allegiance for a very long time.

The most common traditionally recognized measure of dependence, the signs of tolerance and withdrawal symptoms, also fit the model of habitual behaviour I have outlined. Repetition of pleasurable experiences can, over a period of time, be expected to produce signs of changes in neural pathways, or neuroadaptation, which result in withdrawal symptoms. Heavy, long-term cannabis users commonly report a mild withdrawal syndrome of inability to sleep easily, fitful waking sleep for a few days (consistent with cessation of sedative use), vivid dreams (again consistent with disruption of sleep patterns), irritability (common with the breaking of habitual 'comfort' behaviour) and upset stomach, commonly diarrhoea. These soon pass and aren't in the same league as heroin withdrawals, but this does not necessarily downgrade the intensity of hold that cannabis can have. We have, for example, worked with crack users who have found it easier to come off crack than to stop their cannabis use, even though both the experience of using and the experience of stopping use of the two drugs are miles apart.

The final thing to say about cannabis is that, just as it is not as safe as the pro-legalization lobby would have us believe, there is equally no evidence for the 'progression' theory of the right. Progression to other drugs as a result of the pharmacological properties of the substance, or of the inevitable desire to 'try something stronger', simply does not exist. Even in our drug-friendly youth culture, the majority of cannabis users do not go on to use other drugs. It can certainly be argued that cannabis is a 'gateway' into a world where other illegal drugs are more accessible, and therefore that the temptations to try other drugs are stronger. To this extent, it could be fairly stated that cannabis use increases the usage of other substances. In individual terms, however, there is no inevitability about this.

The progression theory is used as one of the main arguments for keeping cannabis illegal; strangely, the risks of cancer do not feature as prominently in the argument, presumably because that line of reasoning is compromised by the legality of cigarettes. Perversely, this may in fact be an argument for just the opposite: by keeping cannabis illegal, are we not therefore keeping the 'gateway' to other drugs open, rather than separating it from the illegal world?

No doubt the debates will continue. No doubt cannabis will continue to be presented, unfairly and inaccurately, as in some way special and different from the other drugs. No doubt the truth will be distorted. No doubt those who even mention the health risks associated with its use will continue to be vilified as reactionaries, and those who point to its therapeutic value – it has potential value with few harmful side-effects in the treatment of multiple sclerosis, glaucoma, asthma, muscular cramps such as period pains and the mitigation of the side-effects of chemotherapy – will continue to be held up as 'traitors in the war against drugs'.

Such arrogant nonsense will continue to make it difficult for us to educate young people about drugs, and to access those who have problems arising from cannabis use. But in terms of hysteria, cannabis has long since lost the ability to generate the kind of panic caused by ecstasy.

Raving about drugs

Young people can, as in a recent well-publicized case, die of combinations of one ecstasy pill, enormous quantities of alcohol and numerous painkillers, and the headlines will be about an ecstasy death. Ecstasy is our new folk devil. It has come to epitomize the threat to our young. It is sold in night-clubs by the unscrupulous to innocent youngsters. You die suddenly from it. It is our nightmare made real. Well, is it? Once again we need to wade through acres of nonsense to get to the truth, and once again we so easily end up confusing and making life more dangerous for young people.

When looking at ecstasy and trying to work out the truth about the drug, it is important to do the one thing that the rave goer cannot do: be sure we are talking about MDMA. At NDAP we have arranged for the regular testing of ecstasy pills to see what is in them, not because we believe that a way forward is to do on-site testing of drugs so that ravers know the quality of the drugs they are buying – both real MDMA and its substitutes have their own dangers – but so that our workers can identify symptoms of distress associated with the maddening variety of substitute chemicals sold as 'E'. Of the last thirty types we have had tested at the time of writing, only two contained MDMA and one the related chemical MDEA. The rest contained combinations or single quantities of ketamine (a drug used in veterinary surgery), selegeline (used in the treatment of Parkinson's disease), ephedrine (nasal decongestant), amphetamines, caffeine, roaccutane (acne treatment) and allereze (hayfever tablets).

MDMA or methylenedioxymethamphetamine, patented in

Germany in 1914, was used by psychotherapists in the USA in the 1970s and, because of the feelings of empathy it produces, found favour in the late-hippy philosophy of the time. In addition to feelings of warmth and intense emotional closeness and empathy towards others and life in general, MDMA has the usual, better-known amphetamine effect of providing a big energy boost. This made it ideal for the growing dance culture surrounding 'warehouse parties' in the mid-1980s, and especially the hypnotic dance rhythms used on the dance scene which grew up in Mediterranean resorts and UK clubs in 1986.

The feeling of abandon, rushes of energy and enormous fellow feeling that taking an 'E' on the dance floor produces fit the drug's name, ecstasy, perfectly. The drug is so popular because the sensations it produces are, in the main, overpoweringly pleasant, and here lies the danger. There is so little about this drug to say 'don't come here again', in fact quite the opposite. Thousands upon thousands of older teenagers and young adults use the drug every weekend at clubs and parties, and society is scared to death. Ecstasy says to its users, 'without any effort on your part you can enter an alternative world which is better than this one, to which this one will never be able to compare'. The very falseness of this world is both its attraction and its danger.

What of the physical and mental health problems, and the deaths associated with this drug? Are they all the invention of a sensation-hungry media, or are young people right to claim that this is a safe drug about which they know more than the medical profession. The truth, of course, is always much more complicated than any stereotype. There are, indeed, many lessons to be learned from the 'E' experience, as much for harm reductionists as anybody else.

Ecstasy deaths began to be identified in 1990, previous to which the bad publicity had centred on the drug's 'mind-altering' qualities. Here the press often confused the effects of 'E' with those of LSD, presumably because of the expression 'acid house', which referred to a particular type of music, and because 'acid' or LSD was more often used in the early warehouse parties. The early deaths were soon identified as being caused by hyperthermia (overheating/

heatstroke). This is turn was attributed to the interaction between the drug and the circumstances in which it was used. MDMA raises body temperature and this is exacerbated when taken in sweaty dance venues. Body temperature is increased further by the drug's ability to keep the user dancing for longer – by 'topping up' on 'E's, dancers can go for around twelve hours non-stop at the all-night venues. MDMA, in common with other amphetamines, also reduces thirst.

Given that young people were likely to continue to take the drug despite any warnings, drugs agencies began to give out harm reduction messages about drinking plenty of water when using MDMA, and about wearing little and loose clothing. Chill-out rest rooms were encouraged, and the advice to dancers was to ignore the messages from the body and remind themselves that everybody requires periodic rests to cool down.

It was also clear that something had to be done in terms of the conditions prevailing inside the club, to which we will return later.

Almost as soon as the harm reduction advice started to circulate, another set of deaths began to occur, this time from hyponatraemia-related problems (dilution of the body fluids). It seemed that the message had been taken on board so universally that even those users who weren't dancing or overheating were drinking large amounts of water. MDMA appears, at least in some people, to depress kidney functions and so reduce the body's ability to eliminate the excess. These factors had combined to result in swelling of the brain (cerebral oedema) and on to coma and death.

Many people seized on these deaths as an argument against harm reduction, and they certainly exposed the weaknesses of using harm reduction as the main thrust of your education strategy when the full facts about what constitutes safer use are not known. Nonetheless, not to give advice about drinking would lead to a return to deaths from hyperthermia, and abstentionist messages would continue to be ignored. For those who use drugs, accurate harm reduction information is essential, no matter how controversial, but we have to get it right.

The problem is that the reporting of cases like Leah Betts has only served to confuse young people. Did she die of an impure 'E'? No.

Then she died as a result of heatstroke? No. She died of too much water? Yes. Then we shouldn't drink water after all? Silence from the press. Advice from the Department of Health: yes and no! We will no doubt find ways in the drugs field of getting the right message across simply and clearly, but we must never suggest that 'safer' drug use means 'safe'. Any chemical is potentially dangerous and a safe drug does not yet exist.

Although death is the publicity-catching aspect of MDMA, given the large numbers of people who regularly use the drug, the figures for deaths are very low, highest estimates being around twenty per year. Harm reduction information, pressure on promoters and venue management to act responsibly, the provision of paramedics, and on-site advice and counselling from services like my own have undoubtedly helped to keep this figure down.

Nonetheless, there are still more deaths from MDMA than from heroin, and many thousands more young people end up in a hospital but survive, usually because first-aid intervention on-site has been speedy. What has been underplayed in terms of publicity and information about the drug is the potential long-term damage to users. A few users have suffered liver damage, but it is the effect on the brain that is causing current concern.

At YAP our counsellors have worked over the past few years with a number of 'E' users who have begun to exhibit disturbing psychological symptoms, often of a long-term nature. These include individuals who complain of 'racing thoughts', a brain that won't rest or think controllably; individuals who have 'rage' reactions and have committed unprovoked and uncharacteristic acts of violence; individuals in significant number who suffer from persistent anxiety or panic attacks; individuals who have become severely depressed; individuals who have begun to interpret every innocuous bodily sensation as a sign that they are dying.

They have several things in common: before they took 'E', they felt normal; they sometimes identified the onset of their symptoms with one single incident with 'E' (although they may have used it regularly beforehand); and they all feel trapped in their own symptoms and their own thoughts and emotions. At first, we didn't associate the symptoms directly with the drug. There was no literature dealing with naturally occurring neuroses. Over a period of time, however, the link has become apparent. Furthermore, research now suggests a possible and disturbing cause for the symptoms.

MDMA causes the excessive release of the neurotransmitter serotonin. This is one of the main factors in the drug creating its desired effect. It appears, however, that the nerve endings in the brain where the serotonin is released are damaged in the process. While cessation of 'E' use allows the damage to the nerve endings to be repaired over a period of time (up to eighteen months in experiments on monkeys), the repairs do not return neural pathways to the original state. As links are re-established, they appear to contain more connections to nearby parts of the brain and fewer to more distant areas. Evidence of research into human brain activity shows the same signs of damage as that in animal experiments. Serotonin levels may also, in the longer term, be seriously depleted. Scientific conjecture is that such damage could lead to depression and even to changes in intellect and personality. Casework from other medical agencies working with 'E' users is beginning to support this hypothesis.

'E' has been, in some ways, a classic example of a chemical trial – without monitoring or evaluation – on a grand scale. Every time someone uses the drug, they are taking part in that trial. The full results we may only find out in years to come, and it is possible that they will be disastrous. On the other hand, it is also still possible that there will be little measurable or permanent long-term damage, but the prognosis is shaky.

We must beware that our desire to defend the freedoms of youth culture and to support young people do not lead us to overstate or argue the case for the harmlessness of chemicals while the jury is still out. To do so harms both individuals and society every bit as much as the repressive over-reactions of the authoritarian right.

The song remains the same

Let us suppose that we get the information right. Even so, whether or not to give it remains controversial. The POST briefing *Common*

Illegal Drugs and their Effects clearly states that '"value-free" information which describes the pleasant effects, and which puts the risk of illegal drugs into "perspective" relative to legal "drugs" such as caffeine, alcohol and tobacco, may end up more of a "which guide" to all the drugs, and a useful check-list of those remaining to try'. While acknowledging that merely negative information is discounted by young people, the authors are still clearly frightened of the contaminating nature of information. It goes on to say of peer education programmes: 'while the programmes have shown promise in a harm reduction context among groups of established drug users, it is more difficult to envisage how they could be used as a drug prevention tool among younger schoolchildren'.

And yet this is clearly contradicted by the evidence of the research into the Youth Awareness Programme carried out by the Home Office, which we referred to in Chapter 3:

> respondents' accounts gave no support for the view that 'if you're not telling them no, then you're saying it's OK'. Although respondents distinguished YAP from the 'just say no' approach, the general messages they took away from the workshops were anti-drugs ones.

The POST report goes on to say that 'the information needs of young people vary greatly'. This is indisputable. At different ages, at different stages of experimentation, use and ex-use, and at different times and in different areas for different drugs, needs will be different, and any 'pupil-focused' education should be sensitive to this. However, POST then goes on to the absolutely extraordinary conclusion that

> Putting together such considerations, leads to the option of providing only a 'safety net' of education to all at school, using the science curriculum to deliver knowledge of drugs' modus operandi, their health and psychological effects; other parts of the syllabus for their legal status and reasons for it ... More detailed information would be made available via other channels to those who have an interest or need ... Other routes through local health and community groups may be more suitable for more 'advanced' briefings on drugs and for harm reduction strategies, and customised access points

might be developed to allow young people to make 'self assessments about stigma, risk, health and dependency prospects', so that they can make more informed decisions about drugs.

So young people are to be taught the science of drugs, which in itself is woefully uncertain and unlikely to make an impression on behaviour, by teachers who, as we have already examined, lack credibility. They are to be taught the law about drugs, which large numbers of adults agree makes little sense in itself – LSD illegal, amyl nitrate legal, ecstasy illegal, ketamine not covered by the Misuse of Drugs Act, tobacco legal, cannabis illegal. And the rest, the social contexts, the questions they want answered, the values, the attitudes and the more 'advanced' information they seek in every class we visit, are to be left to them to seek out at 'customised access points'.

It is not a question of whether young people should or should not receive information. If there are large numbers of 9 and 10-year-olds in most classes who can tell you how to roll a 'spliff' and 50 per cent of 15–16-year-olds have already tried an illegal drug, they already have plenty of information. The question is: who gives them information and messages about drugs – friends, magazines, advertising and drug users, or trained teachers, drugs workers and peer educators?

POST describes itself as providing 'objective and independent information and analyses on science and technology-related issues of concern to Parliament' and then enters the debate by emphasizing an option (the extract quoted above is the only whole paragraph in all 95 A4 pages to be printed in bold) which clearly represents a particular viewpoint held by the authors. It runs contrary to an earlier, more balanced presentation of the merits or otherwise of various different approaches to education in the document.

This unacknowledged bias towards particular viewpoints is shown elsewhere in the document, which is otherwise very valuable and sound. For example, when discussing the legal status of cannabis, the authors state: 'The role of the legal system in the control of drugs is not an issue for this report, but those engaged in the debate may deploy arguments based on interpretation of scientific work on which this review may bear. But then they themselves make statements and interpretations which have little to do with scientific objectivity. The use of bold print, again significant, is included from the original document:

> As discussed ... the evidence on the effect of the legal regime on consumption is equivocal, but **does support the intuitive conclusion that other things being equal, more cannabis is consumed under a 'liberal' regime than a 'repressive' one**. The responses to changes in the regulatory environment may, however, be relatively short-lived, and the ability of a single national regime to depart substantially from the international trends, given the international sophistication of the market, may be questioned.

The bold print shifts the whole emphasis of meaning here. Additionally, the whole argument rather glaringly omits some 'facts' about law enforcement regimes, such as that in the UK, despite harsher penalties and more police and customs resources being spent on enforcement, the drugs trade has expanded on an almost exponential curve.

Now I am not saying which view here is right or wrong. The legalization debate is a complex one, almost certainly hypothetical in nature for the foreseeable future, with many trade-offs. As will have been clear throughout this book, I believe that the debate needs to be held in a calmer fashion and that much more research needs to be done. What I am saying, though, is that finding 'untainted' facts even from those purporting to scientific objectivity is impossible.

While we need always to strive for greater objectivity, we can never totally disassociate 'facts' from the social context in which they are collected and used. We need to be ever vigilant for the hidden agenda, the trace of personal viewpoint. And if we are going to use facts to support a particular purpose, then we need to come clean and say where we're coming from up front.

Giving young people the factual information they require in an unbiased way should be something we always strive for, because not to do so is not to trust them to make rational decisions. Certainly, given the circumstances in young people's lives, there will always be those who use drugs, but this does not invalidate the fact that young people need information they can trust, full information that smacks of honesty, upon which they can base the decisions that they are taking day by day. If they see signs of bias, they will naturally have their faith in both the information and the information giver undermined.

5
Running a young people's drugs service

We have the model for a young people's drugs project that works. We know from research what it looks like and we know from research that it is effective as a model. But what does it consist of in practice? How can it be funded? How does it operate on the ground? How is it staffed, and how are its workers trained to ensure that it remains true to its principles, while at the same time maintaining a profile that is trusted by authorities and funders?

It is only recently that there has been any even remotely significant funding designated to young people's drugs work in the UK. When we established the Youth Awareness Programme in Newham, we were forced to cobble together funding from a variety of sources which on the surface were incompatible in terms of their administrative routes. This led to an impossible management structure for the new service, which in turn made it difficult to attract funding from charitable sources.

Our initial funding came as a Grant for Education Support and Training (GEST) from the Department of Education (as it then was) via the Local Education Authority. This funding was for the post of Drugs Education Co-ordinator (DEC), a post designed to support teacher training already in existence. Changing the post to a management and development role meant close co-operation with the existing street drugs agency in Newham, the Newham Drugs Advice Project. This in turn led to frictions with the Local Education Authority (LEA), which, while supportive to a degree, was concerned to see a member of its staff performing in a new role which it had no experience of managing, and working with the voluntary sector over which it had little control. Initially, progress was difficult owing to the conflicting demands placed upon the post, and things only became easier when positive results started to be shown. But one post does not create a service.

Initial funding for the remainder of the service came in the form of a small grant (£20,000) from the local and newly established Home Office Drugs Prevention Initiative (DPI). DPI was created in the early 1990s, following warnings of the dangers of crack cocaine gaining hold in the UK. A series of meetings with the Metropolitan Police and Drugs Education Co-ordinators at Scotland Yard identified the need to base a new educational initiative in local communities, with the aim of involving and empowering those communities to start to tackle their own problems. For the first three years, selected local authorities were given DPI teams of two workers with around £70,000 per annum to distribute, to develop such community-based initiatives. While the approach was often scatter-gun – let's throw the money at a range of ideas and see which ones produce results – a few promising projects were established.

YAP in Newham was one such project. With the additional funding, NDAP employed a part-time development worker and used what money was left to recruit and begin to train a small team of volunteers, and to produce some high-quality resources to give the new service a clear youth identity. As well as educational 'trigger' materials – a set of cards, one per drug, designed to stimulate discussion – advertising in the form of posters and T-shirts was produced. Young people were involved in every stage of the resource production. Young graphic students from the local Community College did the design work for all initial materials, working to a clear set brief in order to avoid them falling into stereotypical 'anti-drugs' sloganeering. Other young people were involved in the content and wording of cards, posters and T-shirts and in their piloting.

As the service clearly had to be based on volunteers, given the funding available, a careful recruitment programme was begun. Young adults who had been to NDAP for drugs counselling were approached. Because of the climate which sees current drug users as a corrupting influence, they clearly had to be no longer using drugs. They also had to have the confidence to be able to talk to others about drugs without being tempted either to relapse or to use educational sessions with young people as an extension of personal therapy; and they had to be able to keep their own views, either for or against drugs, out of their working environment if we were to achieve the honest impartiality our research with young people had shown was necessary. College students were the other main volunteers in the initial stages. Since, at that stage, we had little to offer them in return, the commitment of the recruits to the philosophy of our work was essential.

Now we had a development worker, some volunteers, some resource materials and the Drugs Education Co-ordinator, but we still had no drugs counsellors who could provide the other, equally important part of the service. This meant that, in the early stages, the DEC and the development worker had to undertake the counselling role, at first with precious little training or support. The counselling could not be delayed for a later start because as soon as the workshop programme began, referrals from and of young people, mainly still at school, started to arrive in numbers.

The problem with a management structure for a service split between the LEA and the voluntary sector was that it made it almost impossible to raise additional funding from charitable sources. Trusts could not understand how such a service could operate, and were prepared to make donations only if the management became unified, which in turn would have cut out one of the existing major funders.

Making the pieces fit

This little history is used here to illustrate a point. With no identified responsibility for funding young people's drugs work, that work has to be developed subversively. One thing that 'Tackling Drugs Together' has not yet achieved is defined responsibility for funding such services. Until these services are in existence, it is easy to argue that there is no need for them. The LEA and health promotion services are tasked with ensuring that treatment services exist, but they will continue to work mainly with opiate-using adults. This is because young people and their drugs are not traditionally accorded treatment priority, because work with adult opiate users is comparatively easy and 'medicalized' (methadone prescriptions and needle exchanges fit nicely with traditional medical models of addiction) and because there is a lot of HIV funding for drugs work which fits injecting drug user services, and comparatively few young people inject opiates (I write this from an East London perspective, aware that in the north-west of England and in Scotland the situation is different with regard to young people and intravenous use).

DPI teams are tasked with 'prevention' in a broader community sense, but here too there is a strong tendency to go for safe, existing models of work. In some parts of the country, DPI teams are contributing funding towards DEC posts for which the Department of Education withdrew funding several years ago. The DPI funding continues regardless of the long history of ineffectiveness of such posts.

Several steps have been taken in the last couple of years by central government in an attempt to point funding in the direction of young people's work. The first was via local DPI teams prioritizing work with young people, but this suffered from the problems outlined above.

The second was through the GEST programme. Following the withdrawal of funding for the DEC initiative, which brought criticism from the Advisory Council for the Misuse of Drugs, the Parliamentary Select Committee and other government departments, GEST was reinstated. However, the main funding was devolved directly to individual schools, usually amounting only to a couple of hundred pounds per school. Many schools 'lost' that money in their main budgets in the first year of the scheme. There was, on top of this, a competitive bidding scheme under GEST, whereby around sixteen local authorities per year were given more substantial sums (usually between £50,000 and £100,000) for 'innovative' projects: it did not commit them to long-term funding and they could redirect the money either at schemes which provided good PR value or towards the current 'big idea' of the politicians. Although it has been involved productively in a number of these GEST projects, and some very good work has been done as a result, YAP does not core-fund basic services. If young people's services were to exist on a competitive bidding, constantly innovating basis, not only would very few exist, but even those few would have to change their whole *modus operandi* every one or two years.

The third attempt to direct money to young people's work came from the Department of Health. Funding was made available to the Standing Conference on Drug Abuse (SCODA) for, once again, 'innovative' schemes aimed at young people. This money only lasted for the financial year 1995/6, which, given the fact that it did not come on stream until July 1995, led to some very short-lived innovations indeed. Again, the whole funding arrangements were 'competitive' between District Health Authority areas, so most localities missed out entirely. For 1996/7 this funding has been announced as 'new money' for District Health Authorities to spend on young people's work.

So we have had the insane situation where three government ministries – the Home Office, the Department for Education and Employment, and the Department of Health – have all plumped for 'competitive' and 'innovative' work with young people. Evaluations are duly published, but to what end? It is no good identifying good practice if it is not to be funded in the long term. We find out what works (sometimes) and then don't have the money to put it into operation.

In 1996/7 the government has made one more attempt to structure funding for young people's drugs services. This is via instructions to the local co-ordinating bodies established under 'Tackling Drugs Together', the Drug Action Teams whose membership consists of the senior managers of the relevant 'big hitter' local agencies in funding terms – District Health Authorities, social services, education departments, police, Training and Enterprise Councils – to prioritize young people's drugs services. At the time of writing, it was unclear whether there was to be any funding additional to the re-routed SCODA money to support the directive. Given the current state of local authority finance, it is hard to be optimistic that anything of major significance will result in terms of providing support for young people nationally in the long term.

Many problems are created by this endless money-go-round. For street agencies, it has become necessary to employ somebody to chase the cash. Where is it going to be this year? What criteria do we have to fulfil to get it? What monitoring and evaluation will there be, and how many reports on progress do we have to write? How can we bring together the different pots of funding, each with its own required outcomes, to form a coherent service along lines which we know are needed and are successful? At times, running YAP has been like being plunged into a Kafkaesque nightmare of bureaucrats, reporters and politicians (most of whom know nothing about drugs, drug users or drugs services), all with their own demands and with immense power. It is grotesque to see so many agencies now suddenly interested in young people, and prepared to 'do down' the opposition in order to obtain a few crumbs of funding, when for years they had shown no interest at all.

For ourselves, we have had to look to unusual sources in order to core-fund the service in the longer term. The training for volunteers, about which more later, has enabled us to tap into funding for job training via the Training and Enterprise Councils (TECs) and the European Social Fund. The outcomes required by such funders have nothing whatsoever to do with drugs work, and the strain of operating in fields with such different requirements – numbers progressing to further education, numbers obtaining employment, numbers gaining qualifications – has at times been close to intolerable, but they help pay for the service we really want to run. European Social Funding operates on a calendar, not financial year. You bid for it after the start of the year it covers, hear whether you have been successful sometime between April and July, and claim the money early the following year when it has already been spent. Money is deducted for every hour a volunteer is late for a training session or is ill, and part of the money is withheld for eighteen months. For a small voluntary sector project, it is a constant skirmish with bankruptcy.

Marketing of drugs training courses to professionals is another source of income. So too are the sale of YAP products like cards and T-shirts. Record sales come next. In fact, the negotiation of sponsorship, marketing and retail deals with the private sector is looming increasingly large as a possible way of ensuring that the funds will be available to underpin a core service which stays true to its initial principles and structure. We are not business people, but we will have to learn that too.

The four young people's projects that YAP currently puts its name to, in Newham, Sutton, Merton and Haringey, are funded by Local Education Authorities, District Health Authorities, probation services, charities, the Single Regeneration Budget, TECs, the European Social Fund, community safety budgets, City Challenge funding, GEST moneys, the marketing of training, the sale of products and donations. And all this to provide young people with essential information, advice and treatment.

Basics

Let us now suppose that we are at the stage where we have obtained sufficient funding for our service. How do we progress? Training for volunteers is the obvious starting point. If a project is truly to represent young people, they have to become, as soon as possible, involved in negotiating and planning their own training. At YAP, our training programme has evolved dynamically through an interaction of agency needs, volunteer needs and available funding. As time has gone by and we have been able to obtain funding for lengthier job training, it has been possible to extend the basic programme to two days per week plus one day per week work experience, and to extend recruitment to unemployed young adults via various employment initiatives, such as 'community action' programmes, and through job centres. Additional recruits have been referred by probation services.

Such young adults have many basic needs which have to be met in order for them to function fully on training courses. These needs are identified via an initial interview and induction process, and may include basic literacy, assertiveness and confidence building, among others. Almost all will need help with writing curriculum vitae and with job interviews. If volunteers are not to be exploited, it is essential that training does not just cover the basic ground needed to run educational workshops. Some agencies pay volunteers for workshops, but this seems to us to be exploitation. Although, naturally, all expenses need to be covered, paying volunteers who are unemployed encourages them to falsify benefit claims and thus puts them in an invidious position. Early on, we decided that volunteers needed to be sufficiently committed to the work not to require direct payment, but that we should seek to accredit or validate their learning. The best way would be through the establishment of National Vocational Qualifications (NVQs) in drug and alcohol work, but as these have not yet been established, alternative credits towards higher education are available via organizations such as the London Open Colleges Federation, and it is these into which we are linking our courses.

Training needs to cover, in a largely verbal and participatory fashion, a broad range of issues. It is essential that volunteers be constantly encouraged to question their own, deeply held attitudes. Drugs knowledge needs to be in-depth, certainly in far greater depth than will be achieved in educational workshops, in order that workers feel confident with their material. As well as basic workshop structures (we have to be sure that workshops delivered by our teams are consistent in terms of information, messages and delivery across the whole organization), the skills required to run the workshops have to be taught. For instance, it is a daunting task for young adults to do classroom work in schools. They need good communication and listening skills, and must be confident in both running workshops and dealing with young people's individual concerns which may arise from them. They need to learn presentational skills and basic role-play techniques ('freeze-frame' role play is a standard workshop method).

Given that our projects are in city areas and that our volunteers come from a wide range of ethnic backgrounds, equal opportunities issues are to the forefront and have to be thrashed out. For example, difficulties for Muslim volunteers with gay issues need resolving during training, not in workshops in front of young people. First aid, rave work and 'chill out' and 'talk down' work for 'E' and LSD users have to be covered to the level of first-aid certificates.

Advanced training for those who wish to stay on at the end of basic training needs to be available. This has to be bought outside the organization and, money permitting, includes counselling, management and outreach training.

All the above requires not only finance, but a great deal of administrative infrastructure and support. All volunteers need supervision, and the structures and staffing to ensure that this is consistently carried out have to be in place. Throughout, volunteers are encouraged to identify their own needs in terms of personal development, and to identify shortfalls in what the agency is offering them.

Getting to young people

The next step, following training, is to gain access to young people. This is not as easy as it sounds. Street and club work may give access to a certain type of involved young drug user, but the many casual users and those who have not yet used drugs are often missed. It is only through schools work that the mainstream can be addressed. And getting into schools can be a nightmare.

Schools may have many concerns in terms of involving drugs agencies in their curriculum and pastoral work. The main one is the impact on the school's image with parents and the wider community. It is easy for positive initiatives to be presented negatively, especially if the school is uncomfortable with the work and presents it in a defensive and apologetic fashion. In our experience, parents are highly supportive of such work if it is presented to them confidently and in advance; it is headteachers who have the greater fears. In terms of publicity, schools which do something about drugs fear being seen as 'having a drugs problem' which they have then had to address. If the publicity comes positively in advance for the school, such fears are not realized.

Another fear for schools is that they will, in some way, lose control of the issue with their pupils. In any case, teachers feel deskilled in this area, many only teaching about drugs because as tutors they have to. They are concerned that the issue will assume an even higher profile and that they will become sidelined and powerless. It is certainly the case that the issue will have a higher profile. Good drugs education opens Pandora's box, much as the issue of sexual abuse became high profile some years ago. The answer with drugs, as with abuse, is not to attempt to drive the issue back underground, but to have a well-trained staff team who know clearly the aims of drugs education, how it fits with outside input, how to follow that input with planned work that teachers feel happy with, and how to deal with pastoral issues that may well arise.

Department for Education and Employment circular 4/95 requires schools to have a drugs policy, covering both curriculum and pastoral issues. We will deal with the pastoral side later, but let us look first at the curriculum issue. Circular 4/95 is a courageous attempt to set a new agenda for drugs education, moving away from 'Just Say No' approaches towards the 'informed choice' model. It includes, in its appendices and in its partner curriculum document, the ideas of *Drugs Education: The need for a new impetus*, produced by the Advisory Council for the Misuse of Drugs. This includes not only primary but also secondary prevention and harm reduction in its aims, and sets drugs education in a social context, calling for the involvement of parents and the wider community in the programme. Circular 4/95, while laying down all sorts of provisos, does talk of the value of outside speakers in educational programmes. The door is firmly opened.

As with everything, training is once again the key. Staff in schools who provide drugs education are normally non-specialists, delivering the programme through Personal, Social and Health Education sessions in tutor groups with limited time. The subject also has low status because there is no examination. There is therefore a tendency to reach for the instant answer, the teaching pack, of which a vast number are currently available. Indeed, there are some individuals who seem to have made a career out of putting variations on the same old exercises in different covers. The problem with teaching packs is that without training for staff they are virtually worthless. It is one thing to provide lesson plans for participating exercises and group discussions; getting them to work effectively is another matter. In order for them to work, staff have to be clear on their aims and practised in teaching methods that are rarely used elsewhere in the curriculum. This can only be achieved through training. Without it, it is easy to fall back on prescriptive and judgmental attitudes which stifle discussion.

Providing this training ourselves, as an outside agency, has been invaluable not only in terms of the quality of teacher-led work, but also in building trust between the agency and schools. It is natural that schools should be wary of young adults with no teaching background coming into their classrooms, often without the teachers themselves being present. Training gives them the opportunity to meet and to view for themselves the expertise and experience of those young people. Programmes of work can be planned together and the workshops run by the 'outsiders' previewed in action.

Effective drugs education will raise pastoral issues. It will lead to young people questioning their own drug use and feeling the need, or at least being open to the possibility, of seeking support or further information. A 'liberal' and open approach in the curriculum will be stifled by an excessively punitive pastoral response to individual use: nobody will have an open discussion about drugs if they feel their comments might result in direct and adverse consequences for themselves. While it might seem far fetched to say that an admission of prior use in a class discussion could lead to punishment, we have known young people to be excluded in just such circumstances for saying that they had once smoked a 'joint'!

Circular 4/95 has a whole section on 'Managing drug-related incidents in schools'. Although it falls between two stools, it can once again be viewed as a positive step forward. The main problem is that it addresses the pastoral issues as a kind of crisis management, responding (as the section heading itself suggests) to individual use when it has become a problem within school. Pastoral intervention should be positive and proactive, holding out the hand of help to young people long before we have got into situations which call for more draconian and punitive responses. The curriculum document says that young people should know where to get help, but this is not enough: the help needs to be on hand, to go to them. The circular gets caught up in issues of informing police and parents when substances have been viewed, at the expense of the extremely positive and sensible concluding paragraphs referring to a 'repertoire of responses' and 'early intervention'.

For a school to take on a drugs counsellor from an outside agency, not only does the school's own confidentiality have to be protected, but a number of other matters have to be carefully considered. Schools which take up such a system need to gain from it: they need to see results in terms of an improvement either in the young person's drug taking or in their performance and behaviour in school. While the second is self-apparent, the former brings up all sorts of confidentiality issues. Feedback from the agency can only be statistical (numbers abstaining, reducing use, using less dangerously, etc.) and therefore only the pupil concerned can give the school the drug-related information it wants, which is obviously problematic. We have found it of great value not only for the counsellor to work through a key member of the school staff, but also for the staff member to meet regularly with a manager from the agency, to monitor and evaluate the work going on.

Other issues for the school include practical concerns. Where will they find a quiet room where counselling can take place uninterrupted? We have held sessions everywhere from stock cupboards to senior staff offices to specially prepared areas. So long as everyone knows where sessions occur, the surroundings only matter in so far as they provide privacy; having a window on to the main corridor is obviously of no use at all!

How will referrals take place and offer at least a degree of confidentiality to the young person? Under our system, pupils can self-refer or be referred by staff. Both raise confidentiality issues. For self-referral, the issue is: how can a pupil either call in on the counsellor at break or lunch without friends knowing, or leave a lesson without both students and staff knowing what's happening?

can be partially overcome by providing lunchtime
ssions offering information as well as counselling, so
son a student calls in is left unclear to those outside. For
ng referred, permission to leave a lesson can be similarly
geneı , making no reference to the reason for leaving the class.
Neither of these systems is entirely satisfactory, however, and in
the end, the success of the system depends on the whole school
understanding the service and respecting the confidentiality issue
on agreed terms.

Despite the problems, we have found that on-site school
counselling, with the agency presenting a supportive and credible
image via classroom workshops, generally proves extremely
successful. It has certainly raised the number of young people
receiving help, in the boroughs where it operates, by up to twenty
times. Those who aren't prepared to use the service in-school know
where to go, through flyers and posters around the school
advertising off-site provision.

While this is not the place to talk in-depth about various
counselling models, one thing has to be made clear: young people
will not sit for an hour while a counsellor uses straightforward
Rogerian methods of summarizing and reflecting back, and the
student generally takes a passive or reflective role. These methods
should be part of the counsellor's toolkit, but young people find
long silences embarrassing, and a more conversational and familiar
approach will have much more success.

The interface

Working in schools requires a major effort on behalf of the agency.
The service has to be sold to management, staff, parents and pupils.
This is a major public relations operation requiring staff training
sessions, parents' evenings, governor training and a professional
image in terms of publicity materials. In fact, a professional
approach to all the work is essential. Secondary schools work to the
bell; being late is a nightmare for the school. Workers must be
sensitive to the constraints and expectations of the school and be

sympathetic to its problems, while maintaining the ethos of the agency. For us this means that our volunteers have to be trained to see the operation of schools from a different perspective from that which they had as students themselves, and to understand educational jargon such as 'key stages' and 'differentiation'.

The schools work benefits greatly, in our experience, from the agency being able to arrive with credibility in young people's eyes which has been established outside the education system. If the agency is known for work in other areas of youth subculture and can arrive with an already established reputation, half the battle is already won. Our work on the rave scene, the direct work at venues, the logo on flyers and tickets, and columns in dance magazines have afforded us a good credit rating with young people. These elements of the service were not, and should not be, created by management. The impetus for such developments needs to come from the talent and enthusiasm of young people themselves, with management staying in the background, providing parameters and a guiding hand.

Working with the 'enemy'

Working on the rave scene has its own difficulties, both practical and ideological. There is no doubt that some rave venues and promoters have no real interest in ridding themselves of drugs in their events; to do so would seriously affect attendance. For most young people, to go to a rave without some form of artificial stimulant would be unthinkable. For a start, it would be very difficult to dance for that long 'unaided'. Ecstasy and speed enhance enjoyment of the event. The club that really did stamp out drug use, even if such a thing were possible, would lose out seriously to its competitors. This is not to condone organizers for turning a blind eye, merely to point out the reality of the situation.

Some unscrupulous promoters have tried to make direct profit from the situation, with doormen searching people on the door mainly to ensure that 'house' dealers make maximum profits inside. Others have turned off the water supply inside so that 'punters' have to buy bottled water to avoid dehydration. This is the nightmare end of the scene and one that can only be tackled by legislation and licence restrictions, but it is clear that even for those trying their best to make a night out 'safe' for young people, there are big problems.

Just to hold dance events invites the accusation of running a drugs den from the press. All such events are, in the 'war against drugs', seen as the province of the enemy. Yet to ban all dancing would be a serious attack on civil liberties and would only drive the drug taking to dangerously remote, unregulated and illicit venues. It would signal a return to the old warehouse parties and to events in fields, with police once again chasing raves around the M25 trying to find out what was going on where.

The obvious answer is to encourage responsible promoters and to work 'with' the problem, rather than against it. We need to recognize that even at events which provide plenty of security, which invite police on to the premises and which ensure the plentiful provision of free water, there will be those who have difficulties arising from drug use. Indeed, the heavier the 'policing' of events inside venues and on the door, the more likely the clientele is to arrive already 'tanked up'. They will go in with dangerously high levels of drugs already inside their bodies, rather than about their person.

Dance venues are, in fact, good places to do drugs work on every level. Tickets and flyers can contain drugs information and telephone numbers of drugs agencies. Drugs workers inside venues can distribute information in print and by word of mouth. Our own rave team has education as just part of its role. Waiting for someone to collapse and be taken to paramedics or on-site first-aiders is to wait until it is nearly too late for the individual in trouble. YAP workers not only are trained in emergency first aid, but also have a strong early intervention function. They carry and provide bottled water. They carry fine-water sprays to cool down overheated dancers. They are trained to spot the first signs of distress and intervene to remind dancers that they need regular rest, despite the high-energy messages coming from drug and body. They can provide massage for those suffering from cramped muscles. They can provide support, advice and counselling for those suffering unpleasant psychological effects from hallucinogen use.

Such a service not only offers dancers a higher degree of safety, it also helps promoters to present a more positive public image and encourages them to maintain good practice. Our service was established by our volunteers, right down to training programmes and to negotiating contracts with promoters. Their involvement made the whole process easier and more effective – they were familiar with the way the whole 'scene' operated and shared a common language with promoters. The thing they found most difficult, and the place where management has a clear and essential role to play, was negotiating sufficiently financed contracts: rave promoters are notoriously 'tight' with money, especially for 'non-entertainment' expenses. The service has worked so well that at some venues we have established a working arrangement with the police whereby, if young people are cautioned or charged with possession, the police return them to the care of our 'counsellors' at the venue, rather than turning them out on the street in the middle of the night.

Running such a service is not just a matter of training workers and then having them turn up. Transport and a non-working driver are essential – if the workers are doing up to twelve-hour shifts 'on a natural' (that is, not taking drugs), you don't want them driving themselves home afterwards. They need equipping with first-aid equipment like rubber gloves and mouth-to-mouth shields, and they need organizing into teams with specific roles and areas of the dance floor to cover. But the benefits are clear. We know that we have been directly responsible for saving a number of lives with this service, and our volunteers enjoy doing it for the informal contact it provides, for the chance to attend the event and soak up the atmosphere, and for the knowledge that they have been of direct help. The relationship between ravers and workers has become extremely positive, as the workers have become more widely seen as being 'on their side'.

In our own case, the direct service has been supported by involvement in writing drugs pages for dance magazines. This stemmed from the good name of the rave service and has become a good vehicle for communicating information about drugs. In youth culture magazines you can use the right 'coded' language, and plug more directly into the ethos of the subculture than you can in formal educational programmes. Writing in this way can provide credibility to quality information. For too long, youth magazines have carried articles which contain plenty of approving references to drug use, but little or no hard fact. Such magazines have seen themselves by and large on the side of the drugs war that is pro-use, and in a way that recognizes little responsibility for their role. Our involvement gives us the chance to redress the balance.

Believe in them

All this has come from giving young people their head. We have many other examples where the interests and enthusiasms of young adult volunteers have led to effective and positive service developments. We are involved in music and recording work, dance schools, graffiti and photography projects, theatre and CD-ROM projects, and much more. Trusting and valuing young people and their culture, and working with and through it, is both valuable and rewarding. But it would all be so much easier if there were recognized responsibility for funding such services, channelled through one clear mechanism and not based on innovation for its own sake. If it works, support it. 'Tackling Drugs Together' and the establishment of Drug Action Teams are a brave attempt to achieve this co-ordinated funding, but until those on the DATs are told rather than encouraged to divert spending in the right directions, and until they have been trained and grounded in an awareness of what really goes on 'out there', and in how empowerment approaches can yield enormous benefits, we will no doubt have to continue to spend six months of the management year in chasing money.

6

The end of the world as we know it

The arrival of 'crack' cocaine in the UK in the late 1980s threw into sharp relief all the problems connected with the bipolar positions of those concerned with drugs issues. Its arrival was prefaced by a visit by a senior representative of the US Drug Enforcement Agency, Robert Stuttman, who delivered stark warnings to the government, police and drugs agencies that crack represented a threat on a hitherto unforeseen scale. At a series of briefings, Stuttman told of a drug with astonishing addictive potential, costing users phenomenal sums of cash to fund their habits, which brought huge increases in attendant crime and prostitution, and for which no treatment currently available was proving effective.

Responses to these warnings produced near hysteria from both conservative and liberal sides of the 'war on drugs'. The moralists went into overdrive in response to this new threat. Conferences such as the Lord Mayor of London's 'Citizens Against Crack' event were called. The police established a special 'crack' squad. Police briefings told officers how to spot a crack dealer and pointed specifically to the black community, identifying black males who drove expensive German cars and were likely to be very polite when stopped and questioned. The liberal drugs field responded by portraying the whole phenomenon as an American scare story designed to support an attack on civil liberties. The Institute for the Study of Drug Dependence produced a leaflet saying that crack was only a problem for those who had previously snorted cocaine. Some drugs experts postulated that the only problem with cocaine, and thus with crack, was that it was expensive – and legislation would soon cure that. This seems to have been a hangover from 1960s medical opinion that cocaine is non-addictive. Drugs agencies across the country said there was no problem; they were not seeing any crack users in their waiting rooms. Black communities warned of crack being an excuse for racist policing.

And the truth? Forgotten once again.

At the time, the Newham Drugs Advice Project found itself in an unenviable position. We already had a few crack users walking through the door, and it was clear to us that the drug represented a new range of problems. The sums of money involved in a crack habit were on a new scale, commonly £1,000 per week or more. Users did not fit the picture of the addict known to a field used to working with heroin users: there were no apparent physical withdrawal symptoms and often there were periods of abstinence between intense binges on the drug. But the craving for crack seemed unusually intense. Many of the clients were having psychotic episodes: one client, for example, had installed electronic surveillance equipment throughout his house in order to prove that while he was at work his wife was making love to a ghost, and he would play us blank tapes as 'proof'. Violence and paranoia seemed to pervade the dealing of the drug. For the first time, many of the users were black, although whites still made up the majority. Traditional treatment methods were proving ineffective. This was clearly a development on the drugs scene which warranted a lot of consideration because it challenged drugs work at its cosy roots. We could no longer deal with docile users who would wait for hours for their methadone prescription. Life was getting difficult.

When we started to announce what was going on, the agency came under intense and vitriolic attack from the rest of the drugs field. We were making it up to get extra funding (although there was no extra funding available for crack work). We were playing into the hands of the right wing. Such accusations were even made in the national press, usually in the middle of articles predicting the end of civilization as we know it.

The danger of rigid priorities

The reasons for such a reaction were clearly more than ideological. If other drugs agencies were not getting crack clients, there had to be a reason. That reason soon became apparent. During the mid-1980s, most funding for drugs work in the UK had been coming from the HIV/AIDS budgets of health authorities, budgets that were fat from the response to the recent hysteria about the new virus. For the drugs field to plug into HIV budgets, it had to show that it was combating the spread of the virus by tackling intravenous drug use – the most clearly relevant method of transmission in the eyes of drugs agencies – and intravenous use usually meant heroin. Heroin users were almost exclusively white and many were nearing middle age. Methadone made life relatively easy for agencies. It was easy money for services which made little effort to look for users; users of heroin went to services in sufficient numbers to keep everybody busy. There was no need to rock the boat. Furthermore, HIV work had finally provided a degree of legitimacy to harm reduction, a concept for which the drugs field had fought long and hard. Crack seemed at the time to be closed to all harm reduction messages: you either used it or you didn't; there was no safer way of doing it.

Crack users found such services unattractive. Whereas they saw heroin users as stereotypical down-and-outs, they saw themselves as sharp, fashionable and highly motivated achievers – 1980s people, not refugees from the 1960s and 1970s. They did not identify with the old picture of an addict, and saw the treatment on offer as having little relevance to them. If they were black, this was compounded by seeing services run by middle-class white people who had no understanding of life on the streets in black communities. For the first time, race and racism were forcing their way on to the agendas of drugs agencies.

Our own agency did not find itself in this unusual position through any proactive initiatives of which we could be proud. We were seeing crack users not because of some exceptional good practice, but because of chance. NDAP was only established in late

1987, long after most other agencies, and we had had the benefit of learning from their experience while the project was being constituted. Built into our constitution was a commitment to work across the whole range of illegal drugs, and to serve all sections of the community of all ages. This did not lead to radically different working methods on the ground: the first staff at NDAP were all new to drugs work and had to learn as they went along. What it did lead to was an open-minded approach to issues, and to the establishment of an image for the service which didn't say to the public 'heroin users, your project needs you'. So the crack users came, and just like we learned about everything else as we went along, so we learned about crack; there was nobody else to learn from other than the clients and a few bits of research from the USA.

The pressure to conform to a party line was nonetheless intense, and it is to the credit of the workers that they were stubborn enough not to opt for the easy way out.

As the years have progressed, we have not had the instant epidemic predicted by Stuttman, but crack use has, nonetheless, reached epidemic proportions among many communities of the urban poor, and is destroying what was left of any quality of life in those areas. Finally, the drugs field had to acknowledge that we were leaders in this country in terms of developing responses.

What do we know now about crack and the reasons for its intense hold? Later we will look at the history of that drug, along with others, at the impact it has had on black communities and at the social implications for drugs services. For now we will concentrate on the effects of cocaine on the body and then on treatment packages.

All around my brain

Cocaine, when taken into the body by whatever means, is taken up by the liver, kidney, heart, brain and fatty tissue. The level in the blood builds up more or less rapidly according to the method by which it is used. If it is snorted, it enters the blood via the nasal membranes, a comparatively small area, and is absorbed slowly,

'It's all a CIA plot, this crack...'

taking between fifteen and sixty minutes to reach peak levels. If smoked in the form of crack, it is quickly absorbed through the surface of the lungs and peaks very quickly, but the effect consequently lasts for a very short period of time – between one and five minutes. For most people the drug is broken down very quickly by the enzyme pseudocholin-esterase into inactive chemicals and is mostly gone within 24–48 hours. Some people do not produce sufficient pseudocholin-esterase, and for them even small amounts of cocaine can be fatal.

Cocaine acts as a local anaesthetic and as a vascoconstrictor, restricting blood flow particularly in small capillaries at the point of entry. Its main effect outside the brain is to activate the sympathetic nervous system which controls the body's fight-and-flight mechanisms, designed to operate when we are in danger. Thus it causes the heart to beat faster, blood pressure rises, body temperature increases, adrenalin pumps, alertness increases, appetite decreases, breathing becomes more rapid, blood sugar levels rise and electrical brain activity increases.

It is the effect of cocaine on the brain that explains the awesome 'hook' of crack. The superficial layers of the brain contain nerve cells, each of which is connected to a nerve fibre, the whole unit (nerve cell plus fibre) being called a neurone. These neurones have many branches which receive incoming signals from other cells. The area of interface between two nerve cells is called a synapse, a small gap. This gap is commonly bridged by chemical compounds called neurotransmitters. The main neurotransmitters in the case of cocaine are norepinephrine and dopamine. In simple terms, when a message comes down the nerve cell, the sending cell spills neurotransmitters into the synaptic gap. The neurotransmitters then attach to specialized receptor sites on the cell receiving the message. This causes the next cell to 'fire' or not to 'fire'. Following this, the neurotransmitters are released back into the synaptic space, where they are broken down by enzymes or returned to the original cell to be broken down. The latter process is called 're-uptake'.

Cocaine appears to stimulate the release of norepinephrine and dopamine in neurones involved in the regulation of consciousness, attention and arousal. It also appears to block the re-uptake of these neurotransmitters and so interfere with their breakdown, so increasing their availability in the synaptic gap. The tendency of the user to repeat the cocaine experience is attributed to the effect of dopamine on the pleasure centres of the brain, which means that 'addiction' to cocaine is caused by the pursuit of euphoria rather than the avoidance of drug withdrawal. This is the 'craving' so notable in crack users and accounts for 'bingeing' followed by periods of abstinence without physical withdrawal symptoms.

Another common feature of prolonged cocaine use is the compulsive repetition of often meaningless activities, particularly those requiring attention to detail. Over time, damage to nerve pathways regulating movement starts to occur, and this may result in slowed movements, staring and users adopting bizarre postures. In the limbic system, the part of the brain regulating emotion, this damage may lead to behavioural changes and even to seizures. One of our clients suffered a seizure which caused him to snap his own teeth with the muscle tension involved.

Cocaine reinforces itself by sensitizing the neurones and thus making the user able, over a period of time, to experience excitatory effects from smaller doses of the drug. Cocaine also triggers the reward mechanisms of the brain and floods it to the extent that all other pleasures and rewards lose their meaning. The user therefore returns again and again to seek the rewards of the drug, and drifts away from lesser rewards that have to be striven for uncertainly, such as those obtained from work and relationships.

As cocaine leaves the body and brain very rapidly when smoked as crack, the euphoria turns to dysphoria very quickly and this is described as the 'crash'; users liken the feeling to that of falling off a cliff. This in turn feeds the desire to use again, and contributes to the sort of binges that continue until the money or the drug is gone. As the drug works directly on the brain, rationalization of the process does not help the user to resist use, merely to make excuses for the behaviour. However, the more the user returns to crack during a binge, the euphoria decreases each time, but the craving continues. The pulse begins to race, the chest begins to ache and paranoia sets in. Often at this stage the user will seek heroin or tranquillizers to temper the undesirable effects of the drug; they will seek a 'parachute' to bring them down gently. This can lead to secondary or multiple dependencies.

As the drug runs out at the end of a binge, the crack user experiences intense anxiety and often has delusions that there is more of it about somewhere. 'Scanners', as users in this stage are called, will search the floor for minute specks of the drug that they imagine are spilled. Body temperature is high and heavy sweating occurs.

Soon after this, within an hour of cessation of the binge, the craving decreases and remorse sets in. Hunger and tiredness return with a vengeance. Well-intentioned desires to cease use and get treatment are common at this point.

A day later, relief takes over, together with a more positive feeling about life. They have handled it. Life is getting back to normal. They have no withdrawals. They are one of the ones who can handle the drug. There may be a restless emptiness about life, but this is not a withdrawal symptom. This flatness or depression is thought to be caused by a reactive shortage of norepinephrine in key areas of the brain. Users feel that they have overcome their cocaine problem. Because their problems are no longer consciously appreciable, users believe they have gone away.

In fact they remain lurking in my subconscious

An association or reminder of the drug, often days or even weeks later, will trigger off cravings once again. There are now two possible routes: treatment or another binge. Anything can act as the next binge trigger – proximity to the drug, memories of using, meeting other users, a song they heard while bingeing, or a crumpled can such as those used to make home-made pipes. The craving becomes overpowering and the user becomes fixated on obtaining more crack. They will do anything necessary to get it; they feel driven. Anticipation occurs; users get a dry mouth and a racing pulse, imagining the drug's effects. In the East End this is called 'going on a mission'.

With heavy long-term users, paranoid psychoses are common, although they may occur in some individuals with relatively low levels of use. This psychosis creeps up via periods of increased suspiciousness, compulsive behaviour and dysphoria. Irritability and fault finding occur. Gradually, delusional thoughts take over, of the types described earlier. Hallucinations and persecutory 'voices' are common. Everyday events are interpreted as supporting the delusional beliefs. This combination of feelings may lead to violent behaviour against imagined 'persecutors'. Such psychosis may be explained by continuing high levels of dopamine in the brain.

The psychosis is very difficult to distinguish from certain types of schizophrenia. Indeed, individuals under stress or with an underlying psychiatric disorder are particularly prone to full-blown psychoses from crack use.

Crack smoking has a number of other damaging effects. The constricting effects of smoked cocaine on blood supply affect the vocal cords, causing voice problems. The smoke irritates the airways of the lungs, causing damage to these delicate parts and sometimes causes infections, bronchitis and pneumonia. Increased pressure caused by deep inhalation may force air through small tears in the lungs and into the space around the heart, where it can cause disturbances in the heart rhythm. Sometimes death may occur as a result.

Such disturbances to the rhythm of the heart are the most common complication from the use of cocaine. Additionally, large doses decrease the heart's own blood supply and may cause heart attacks.

Cocaine is toxic to muscle tissue, potentially causing cramps in any muscle group, and large doses may also overload the liver, causing damage to that organ.

It is not surprising, given this list of its effects, that crack has had such a dramatic impact on certain areas or communities. It offers the allure to dealers of easy money; it is hugely profitable. By the same token, given the intensity of craving and the enormous cost to the user, it is not surprising that drug-related acquisitive crime rises rapidly in areas where crack is prevalent.

In Newham in 1989–90, we found ourselves in the eye of the storm. For the first time we faced a blatant and active street dealing scene in the area, operating 24 hours a day, 365 days a year. For those with little future, dealing crack seemed to offer a way out, but as we shall see in Chapter 7, this turned out for most to be an illusion. Violence began to surround the dealing scene with guns becoming common, even for some low-level cannabis dealers scared of having their drugs or money forcibly removed by those on the crack scene. The dealing squabbles became irrational, paranoid and violent. Feuds developed over perceived double-dealing or grassing. Crack clients at the project were often agitated, paranoid and, occasionally, aggressive. In the main this aggression was verbal, but on a couple of occasions we had to deal with potentially nasty incidents in the waiting room. Clients would give out unsolicited information in counselling sessions, and when a bust occurred, this might point to the worker as the information source. Previously, our strict and well-publicized confidentiality policy had been enough in itself to discourage such thoughts, but rationality was not the order of the day.

There must be some way out of here

Without any established treatment packages that were proving effective, we were forced to develop our own, first by studying any available literature from the United States and then through a trial-and-error approach. Initially, there seemed to be two avenues from the States worth exploration. The first, the use of tricyclic anti-depressants, proved to be a short-lived hope. Trials were carried out at the Maudsley Hospital in London under Dr John Strang and the anti-depressants were found to be ineffective in combating craving, the main feature of dependency. The claim made for acupuncture, that it could be a cure in itself, also proved to be overstated. Nonetheless, through developing a relationship with a local practitioner, acupuncture did prove to have its uses.

When crack users arrive at a treatment agency, they are very commonly in an agitated state, either just 'crashing' or at the beginning of the next craving. This is not a desirable state in which to begin counselling. The user needs to be calm and reflective, not excited and driven. Acupuncture proved to be very effective in providing a window in which to calm clients, often lasting 24–48 hours. The practice developed into sending clients for acupuncture one evening and arranging their counselling sessions the next day. Later, we found a number of 'alternative' therapies, such as aromatherapy and shiatzu massage, to be similarly beneficial. This pattern of therapy and counselling, therapy and counselling, proves effective long into the treatment process and after cessation of use. But how does it work? While much is still unclear, it is postulated that acupuncture releases endorphins and dopamine into the brain and helps to re-establish some sort of equilibrium.

Acupuncture is practised in the West using only part of the whole medicinal and spiritual philosophy on which it is based. In Chinese medicine, the term 'xu huo' (empty fire) refers to the lack of inner calm which allows the fire of aggression to burn out of control. At this stage, however, we were interested only in the immediate effects of the treatment and looked no further. The part to be played by the 'bits we left out' will be considered in Chapter 7. One thing, however, is clear. Acupuncture and other alternative therapies bypass the conscious and have a direct, positive effect on the brain, emotions and physical sensations, and on related behaviour.

New clients may find that they need a 'way in' to discussing their behaviour in a psychological fashion. There is often an initial resistance to treatment or a denial of the problem; clients often say that that are attending to satisfy friends, relatives, spouses or the criminal justice system. Acupuncture and other therapies provide a way of retaining clients by avoiding the need for immediately intense client–counsellor relationships. The user feels immediate benefits and becomes gradually more open to therapeutic counselling relationships. Clients who can't even trust themselves, let alone a counsellor, find that the re-establishment of an inner calm enables them to understand and put more faith in their case worker. The process enables the worker to harness the energies of the 'troublesome' client to the achievement of more positive goals.

In this calmer and less resentful atmosphere, clients can be helped to set their own goals and to make their own choices – a philosophy of empowerment which is central to the work of our agency.

Another benefit of acupuncture is that it works directly on the 'now' rather than on past pains and experiences, or on future needs. It is in the 'now' that each of us exists, and we cannot deal with the past or the future when the present is placing a barrier of anxiety, paranoia, aggression, guilt and other emotions in the way. The past and the future are the province of the counsellor. The present is resistant to counselling, but open to alternative therapies; the reward is immediate – a situation crack users seek and are familiar with.

Before we can 'lock on to' a client using acupuncture, however, we have to deal with the agitated person on a first visit who feels impatient and disbelieving of any kind of treatment package. Crack clients will not wait for hours to be told that talk is all they will get and that recovery is a long process. They need to be grabbed, to have their attention caught by some mechanism. We soon found at NDAP that the first few minutes of contact were vital to retention of clients. This, we discovered, could be achieved by offering clients a factual description of the way a drug made people feel and act, allowing them to recognize similarities with their own emotions and behaviour. Then the worker would need to lay out a 'stall' of what we had to offer and how it would help. Making things concrete with calm assurance enabled clients to believe that the worker understood the drug and that a clear set of 'things' would happen to achieve a desired result. An appointment for acupuncture would be made at the first meeting, so that the initial 'hook' would be followed quickly by the 'line'. 'Things' were thus happening very quickly and with noticeable effect.

Counselling with crack users, following the use of alternative therapies, could then begin to unpick the roots of the dependent behaviour, examine underlying issues, relate these to present patterns of thought, emotion and action, and identify courses for future action. One of the key areas to be addressed with crack users is how the feelings of supreme self-esteem and power engendered by the drug fulfil a function for that individual.

Later we will look at how history, socioeconomics and psychology combine to make some sections of the community more susceptible to the siren call of the 'rocks', but here we will stay more generally illustrative. A low sense of self-worth is common to many people; this may be as a result of parental attitudes, bullying, marital problems, unemployment or a host of other factors. Crack offers a temporary but immediate escape from such a self-image – the user is transformed into a superhero for a while. If they are to free themselves from the hold of the drug, one of the central tasks for users is to identify the origins of low self-opinion in themselves, address it, re-evaluate their experience through the eyes of the present, and rediscover a sense of personal pride or love of self (and thus of others) that will help to overcome the need for an artificial aid. For someone to stop using a drug, the function that the drug fulfilled in their life has to be replaced or satisfied by some alternative means. If the drug is used as a way of coping with some aspect of reality, then other coping strategies must be developed.

Women on the rocks

Let us illustrate this by looking at the particular attractions of the drug for women.

Women currently constitute about 50 per cent of crack users, an unusually high figure for any drug. There may be a number of reasons for this, among them exploitation by male users or dealers and pimps who see the drug as an easy way to exert power over women, and use them to make money or provide easy sex. It may be that, for women with problems, crack offers a more attractive method of use than the bodily intrusive practices of intravenous heroin use. What is clearly true is that, given the lowly role and status of many women and the unrealistic pressures placed upon them by society to look like catwalk models, to be carers and perfect mothers, to bring in an income and to be sexual superwomen, crack offers them a particularly alluring package. The drug promises immediate transportation from any starting position their feelings may be in, to feelings which equate with those they might expect superwoman to have: energetic, fast thinking, powerful and able to deal with any problem. Because of its appetite-suppressing effect, it even makes the pounds fall away. All this in an instant. The love for crack ascends to greater levels than anything else in life, and crack is a harsh lover.

When the crash comes, the feelings of power are replaced by guilt. Women are carers, therefore they must think of others first. Who have they wronged by their behaviour? Their children? Their family? Their partner? Such guilt can be overwhelming, and the easiest method of escape is to go back to being superwoman again and to smoke some more crack.

Unless these issues and processes are identified and addressed, there is little chance of a woman freeing herself from the cycle of use, euphoria, crash, guilt, and use once more. The crack lifestyle is especially dangerous for women. The easiest and fastest method for a woman to finance a crack habit is prostitution. The more desperate you are for an immediate hit, the greater the temptation to agree to unprotected sex and other high-risk sexual activities, with the consequent risk of contracting sexually transmitted diseases, including HIV. Crack dealing/using culture is in itself highly volatile. It is very easy for women to get involved, to feel powerful enough to handle any situation and then to find out that the real power is not with superwoman but with superman.

The role of woman as carer makes access to help even more difficult for women. Women who use crack during pregnancy run the risk of miscarriages, premature births, babies born underweight, and fractious and irritable babies. This brings feelings of guilt which may lead to denial: I have harmed my child before it is even born – nobody must know – I must not know. In the USA, mothers who use drugs during pregnancy have been charged with all manner of offences, including child abuse, drug distribution to minors, criminal neglect, contributing to the delinquency of a minor, and involuntary manslaughter.

It is clear that what is in operation with regard to pregnant users is a combination of prejudices against drug users and prejudices against women. Representative Bishop of the Pennsylvania House of Representatives has asked, 'should smoking, drinking alcohol, exposing oneself to contaminants in the work place, or staying on one's feet too long also be subject to criminal penalty?' Many activities that women have to perform could be regarded as injurious to a child's health, and social deprivation and poverty are clearly potentially dangerous to the unborn because of their effects on health and nutrition. Indeed, it could be argued that taking pregnant women through the courts and into prisons is just as likely to injure the unborn child; the punishment may be as dangerous as the crime. Such legal moves have little to do with concern for the unborn, but much to do with society exacting revenge on the 'fallen woman'.

While such legal positions do not exist in the UK at present, they are indicative of the judgmental attitude of authority towards women, which makes them justifiably nervous of seeking help for a drug problem. Women with children are reluctant to use services for fear of having their children taken away by social workers. Even if they seek help, there exists a lack of services catering for their needs – crèches in street agencies, spaces for children in rehabilitation centres, refuges and space safe from harassment.

Treatment packages therefore need to deal with all these issues if they are to begin to cater for a crack-using clientele.

So now we have a quick, concrete introductory meeting, acupuncture and other alternative therapies, counselling designed to identify underlying feelings of inadequacy, to address them and to identify ways forward, and facilities, policies and procedures designed to meet the needs of different client groups and to make longer-term attendance easier for them. But this is not enough.

Constant craving

Counselling must also help crack users to develop strategies for dealing with craving and with their 'trigger' mechanisms – the ideas and experiences which have an association with or provide a reminder of the drug, and which spark off their cravings. Some of these triggers may be very real aspects of the user's life. For example, if you live in the area where you buy your crack, you will probably be surrounded daily by physical reminders of the drug together with easy access: your dealer lives in a house that you pass every day; the people you smoked with are on the street around you every day; you had a binge at this address and so on. There is only one way to avoid contact with these triggers and that is to move out of the area. For most users this is not a realistic option, although for some it represents a difficult but workable strategy. On the surface, a period in a rehabilitation centre offers a quick solution, but in fact it often offers false hope.

While it may be easier to make a lengthy break from the drug and all its connections in a setting away from temptation, given the long-term hold of crack in terms of its effects on the brain, the tendency to craving takes a very long time to subside. Having a period of fewer triggers for craving may be very useful in the short term, but it can lead to a false sense of security, the 'I have beaten it' syndrome. Eventually, however, the individual has to return to the old surroundings, and all too often the sudden pulling of triggers overwhelms them and they quickly return to using.

The delay in accessing rehab can, in itself, be enough for agencies to lose crack users. Arranging funding can take weeks, unless fast-tracked as a crisis intervention, and crack users are impatient either for results or for crack. You have to be drug free on admission. If you drop out of the programme, it is usually several months before you are permitted to try again. Spaces are few and are filled quickly. Many are used to dealing with heroin users and offer no crack service.

On the other hand, staying in the community means that the triggers are all around and progress may be very difficult. There may be many relapses and, without careful handling by the counsellor, it is easy for a feeling of hopelessness to set in. Imagine this scenario. A 13-year-old crack-using prostitute from a brutal family background is identified by her school as in desperate need of help. Over time, she has gained what self-esteem she has from her reputation as a rough girl, looked up to by many because of her lack of respect for authority and given 'respect' out of fear.

She has hangers on, other rough girls, who live off her reputation and are keen to stay with her group. She has a 19-year-old pimp and dealer, although she wants to believe he loves her and she has lacked love since a young child. Everyone she knows is involved with the crack scene, using, dealing or hustling. There are no rehabs that will take her because of her age. Coming away from crack for her in the community will obviously mean a very difficult and almost total reorientation of her life.

Once the girl has been through assessment and begun acupuncture, the counsellor will need to look at the roots of her low self-esteem, but this will be made more difficult because even when they are identified she will still be living at home and constantly undermined, punished and denied the love she craves. She will have to find self-worth in some other way. This may include joining self-help groups and getting involved in some positive activity at which she will gain success and praise. It will certainly involve a major shift in self-perception. While this is going on, she will have to deal with the constant triggers to craving and use, and this will inevitably involve a complete detachment from all her old associates. Any such move on her part will lead to resentment from the 'boyfriend' and other people in her group, and there will certainly be a great deal of unpleasantness and possibly even violence towards her.

These relationships will also have to be replaced by others, and where are they to come from? Again, support and self-help groups, preferably task-oriented groups, may prove invaluable. And then, what is she to do with the time she used to spend on the crack scene? School may, on the surface, provide some structure to her day, but it is likely that her behaviour will have provided her with a backlog of ill-will from staff. Her grip on a school play may be tenuous, and any bad behaviour will be judged in the light of past incidents.

She has, by law, to receive education, so a package of treatment, counselling, day care and education at a pupil referral unit will probably provide the best solution. This costs money (although not as much as the cost of rehab or of letting her continue into the criminal justice system) and has to be worked out between the agencies concerned. Many day-care centres for drug users will not work with people so young. Even if they do, she faces a massive struggle, and motivation and the formation of new friendships which will positively occupy the evenings when she used to walk the streets are overwhelmingly important.

On the other hand, the benefits of coming off while remaining in the community are potentially enormous. If users can face their problems and learn to cope with triggers while remaining in the environment, the results are likely to be much longer lasting. Users will know that they have achieved, and can continue to achieve, major changes in their life in the face of the strongest adversity. The effect on their self-esteem will be massive and, provided they continue to receive support through any subsequent traumas or difficulties, should see them through to a productive future.

Any productive future will need to involve work. In inner cities work is scarce and there is fierce competition for jobs. Employers will not look favourably on those with a history of drug use and crime, with no training or qualifications, and no history of employment. Real employment training therefore becomes a key issue. Crack users, like other drug users, often find college courses or training schemes intimidating or difficult to cope with. They are used to instant gratification, not working for long-term rewards. It is therefore essential that drugs services develop specific initiatives to deal with this problem.

At NDAP we came to tackle the problem in two ways. Our day-care service, Vital, offers a range of training in basic skills for the workplace, in a setting where support is constantly on hand. This support includes on-site alternative therapies, trained drugs workers and counsellors offering individual support, plus access to 'women and crack' and 'men and crack' support groups. These groups are self-directed, but are supported by trained staff. Support groups for ex-users are also task oriented; their role is to produce information resources about the drug for users and to act as an information base on crack and related issues for the whole organization and for other agencies.

The second training initiative was described in Chapter 3: the volunteer training course for the Youth Awareness Programme. Through this, ex-users can not only learn in-depth about drugs, and thus come to understand them better, but also cover much broader issues relating to work in the drugs field and caring professions, while gaining accreditation.

By becoming involved in the education programme for young people, they can turn the negative experiences of their past to positive use, with consequent gains in terms of their own self-esteem and self-confidence. They discover that they have abilities and knowledge that are sought after, and that they can play a productive and valued role in society.

So we can see that working with crack users presents drugs services with a number of challenges: interventions have to be quick and efficient in order to catch clients when the opportunity arises; counsellors have to understand the drug and have strategies to deal with triggers and craving; a range of alternative therapies have to be easily and speedily available; a continuum of care has to be provided, including support groups and training schemes; and packages of support and care need to be developed with other agencies, all ready to be accessed relatively quickly.

Although we knew as early as 1990–1 roughly what kind of provision was necessary, it took us until 1996 to gain sufficient funding to have most of the components in place, although we still lack funding for a full-time crèche and for necessary outreach work. Our task now is to make them all fit together and work efficiently and effectively in the clients' best interests. Many areas are still fighting for funding and services, and having to get by as best they can with not very much. Even where a full range of services is available, crack remains the drug which is most difficult for clients to stop using and stay away from.

We know individuals who have not used crack for three or four years, who still say that on occasion they can taste the smoke in their throat, who daydream about the drug and have to fight periodic craving.

The tragedy once again is that the squabbling of the various factions which resulted from the postures adopted during the 'war on drugs' left the field paralysed for so long. Right from the start what was needed was a co-ordinated programme of research looking at the pharmacology, neurology and effectiveness of different treatment options. Instead we had a combination of uncoordinated law enforcement and education packages, and a drugs field which could 'see no evil, hear no evil, speak no evil'.

As a result, we lost years in coming to grips with the problems posed by crack, and the drug has got a much greater hold in our cities and in different communities than it need have. We have to hope that the lessons have been learned for the next time, which will surely come, but I rather suspect that we will find ourselves once again posturing and pointing fingers across an ideological divide.

One lesson it is essential for us all to learn has been thrown into sharp relief by crack, and it is an issue which will be addressed next in this book: we cannot allow racism to govern our responses to drugs.

7

Soul on ice

I take my freedom lest I die
for pride runs through my veins not blood
And principles support me so that I
With lifted head see liberty, not sky
I am he who dares to say
I shall be free or dead today. (Mary Evans)

We cannot begin to understand the special problems that a drug like crack poses for black communities, unless we understand how black culture and sense of self have been devastated by colonialism and racism, and how race and drugs have been destructively linked for at least a century. If we cannot understand these issues, our services will continue to be underused by people of colour and our treatment programmes will continue to be less than effective for drug users from these communities.

Since the earliest days of the slave trade, associations have been made between black people and the drug trade. This is not to imply that when the slave traders arrived in Africa they found people with drug problems and transported those problems to the Americas with the slaves. It is true that alcohol and other mood-altering substances were in use in Africa at this time, but, as with all close-knit cultures that had had centuries to understand and accommodate substance use, there existed a tradition of appropriate use. Substances were used for ritual and for healing, and when used for pleasure they were used moderately. Social norms for use were long established and observed. It was the activities of the trading companies themselves which began to disrupt norms of use and to transport and transplant drugs to different parts of the world where these norms and traditions had no meaning. Slaves were traded for rum and tobacco. Although slaves in the Americas were allowed limited access to alcohol, for example, the African tradition of moderation persisted for a long time. Hemp was brought to the USA and the Caribbean by slave traders, where it formed the foundation of the soon powerful rope and cloth industries. Its medicinal properties were learned from African culture, and cannabis soon became used for these purposes by white Americans.

The transplantation of substances managed and accommodated by one culture to other unprepared cultures as a result of trade has a long history of devastating consequences. Coca leaves chewed by Andean Indians without problems for centuries have become the cocaine problems of other cultures with no tradition of appropriate use. Colonial trading companies exported opium to countries with no tradition of use across Asia and the Far East, and created enormous problems. Far from showing concern, the trade was supported by the use of force. The opium trade led to today's heroin problems in western countries.

Western priorities

It was only when problems of heroin and cocaine addiction began to affect middle-class white people that the authorities started to take an interest in imposing restrictions, and even then the measures that were taken had as much to do with power, foreign policy and global interests as with tackling the problems.

When Austrian chemist Albert Niemann sythesized pure cocaine from the coca plant in 1860, the drug's energy-enhancing properties were capitalized upon by the medical profession and commercial interests. By the late 1800s, pharmaceutical companies such as Merck and Parke Davis became involved in importing and dispensing cocaine. Initially the trade was unregulated and cocaine was sold door to door. Cocaine-based products included cigarettes, tablets, ointments, teas and liquor. A number of soft drinks containing cocaine appeared, including Coca-Cola.

By the turn of the century, opium and cocaine addictions had reached such levels among white Americans that anti-drug campaigns sprang up. There is no evidence of significant use of these drugs by black Americans at this time. Drugs laws began to be introduced in the USA in 1906 with the District of Columbia Pharmacy Act and the Pure Food and Drug Act. By 1909, when President Theodore Roosevelt appointed Dr Hamilton Wright to lead a commission to an international conference on stopping the opium trade in Asia, both the importation of opiates and the number of opium addicts were decreasing.

The real goal of the politicians, however, was to increase US influence in the Far East, and therefore it was necessary for the USA to take the lead in introducing restrictive legislation in order to get other countries to follow suit. Getting such laws introduced required dishonest tactics. Dr Wright therefore greatly exaggerated statistics on the scale of the problem. His *Report on the International Opium Commission* particularly exaggerated the scale of drug use among blacks.

This report is the first widely known example of the use of racist propaganda to push through a policy on drugs, but it was certainly not to be the last. Wright's report played on white fears and prejudices by claiming that cocaine gave blacks superhuman strength, sent them into extreme states of madness and drove black men to rape. The tactic was successful and resulted in the Harrison Narcotics Act of 1914.

By the 1920s and 1930s, the same tactic was being used to legislate against cannabis. Again, there were economic rather than health reasons behind the desire to stop the trade in cannabis. The main attacks on cannabis came from the Hearst newspaper empire as well as in pulp fiction. Hearst saw the use of hemp as a high-quality substitute for paper as a direct threat to the lumber and newspaper industries that he controlled. He coined the term 'marijuana' to disguise the fact that his attack was on the hemp plant and the rapidly expanding growth of hemp as a crop in the USA. Hearst was also a racist and, building on the approach taken by Dr Wright, set his media empire to work creating racist scares about the use of marijuana by blacks. Sex, race and drugs were used to touch the psyche of white Americans.

Interracial sex was a cause of hysterical fear among whites. Building on racial stereotypes of the sexually potent black male, Hearst publications produced tales of white women seduced into sex and drugs by blacks who had had their sexual desires driven out of control by marijuana use. Marijuana gave blacks extraordinary strength and promoted violent sexual desire.

The man who drove through the legislation for the authorities was Harry J. Anslinger, the racist director of the Federal Bureau of Narcotics from 1930 to 1962. Anslinger testified to Congress that 'coloureds with big lips lured white women with jazz and marijuana'. The 1937 Marijuana Tax Act, which outlawed the drug's use and sale, marked the success of this concerted campaign. The image of 'drugs equals blacks' was now firmly entrenched in public consciousness. The war on drugs was clearly a war against particular groups in society.

However, it was not just a case of legal policy using race as a tactic. Racism ran through all sections of society, including the crime syndicates. After the Second World War, the Mafia could see that, just as prohibition of alcohol had offered them great commercial opportunities in the 1920s, so the prohibition of drugs could make them even greater fortunes. However, even to the Mafia the sale of narcotics posed a moral dilemma because drugs were regarded as undermining their traditional morality. This dilemma was causing trouble between the 'families'. In the end a compromise was reached to satisfy all parties: the mob would only sell drugs to blacks. By the 1950s, the drugs trade on the East Coast of the USA was controlled by the Bonanno, Gambino, Genovese, Lucchese and Procaci-Maglioco families.

Very quickly the black communities were facing a heroin problem of enormous proportions.

Don't give it to my brother

In response to this problem, an organization called the Nation of Islam grew to offer a serious alternative lifestyle. The Nation identified drug use as an attempt by blacks to escape or blunt the hurt of racism, and proposed membership as a way for black people to rediscover their self-esteem. The role racism plays in drug use by individual black people will be looked at later. For now it is sufficient to note that the relationship between drugs and racism in terms of the individual and their recovery was first defined by a black organization that grew from the community it served. Malcolm X himself was originally a drug dealer.

In order to get drugs into the black community, the Mafia also had to recruit from that community. It was inevitable that at some point there would be an attempt by those blacks essential in running the Mafia's business to take over the trade. In 1967 Frank Matthews went independent from the mob and began to control a big part of the black street trade. He was replaced in the early 1970s by Nicky Barnes. During this time the Vietnam War was turning thousands of black servicemen to drugs. The stress of the war, which was having a similar effect on servicemen of all cultural groups, was compounded for blacks by racism within the armed services. Heroin and cannabis were easy to obtain in Vietnam and the US authorities made no serious efforts to stop trafficking or provide treatment.

Indeed, the CIA was busy working with criminal and anti-communist groups in Laos, Myanmar and Thailand (the Golden Triangle) who were involved in the drugs trade. The CIA armed, supplied and trained groups in the region and in return bought the opium crop. As the USA pulled out of Vietnam in the early 1970s, traffickers in the region began shipping large consignments of heroin to US cities. During the war heroin imports from the region increased from 8 to 60 tons a year.

With the notable exceptions listed above, control of the drugs trade still rested with those with money, power and the ability to launder profits discreetly, and these people were still, in the main, white. Nonetheless, the decay of the inner cities and the attacks on welfare projects by the Reagan administration of the 1980s were leading to the involvement of black youth gangs in running lower-level dealing. With mass unemployment there were plenty of volunteers to do the job. Before long 'turf wars' began over who could deal where, and black-against-black violence became a major feature of the scene. Whether this situation was just allowed to develop by authorities that didn't care because the drugs trade was now a geopolitical weapon, or whether, as many black organizations argue, there was a conspiracy to make it happen, is still the subject of much debate. What is indisputable is the effect of the drugs epidemic on black communities in the cities, in terms of crime, violence and the descent into deeper poverty. It is interesting to note that many right-wing politicians who claim that drugs are a moral issue cite drugs as the cause of disintegration of inner city communities rather than a symptom of social and economic deprivation. Currently one in four black males in their twenties in the USA are somewhere in the criminal justice system. Punish the victims again.

It was left to the black communities themselves to fight back. The Black Panthers outlawed the use of drugs other than cannabis among their members, seeing it as undermining the growing political consciousness of black people during the 1950s and 1960s. We shall return to this issue in more depth when we come to consider drug use in the black communities in the UK. The Nation of Islam runs patrols to get rid of dealers in Washington, and couples this with free counselling and treatment programmes. In another part of Washington the Fairlawn Coalition is also involved in patrolling the streets.

It can be seen from this brief history that black people have been used by the drugs trade and politicians to further economic and political goals. They have been labelled and scapegoated. They have their communities destroyed. But they still control little of the trade above the lowest levels and still form the minority of users. Yet this is not the view of drugs and blacks that the majority community holds. In the popular consciousness, blacks are still seen as mostly responsible for the drugs problem.

The picture in the UK

Now let us turn to the situation in the UK and review the arrival of crack cocaine and public responses to it in the light of this history. We will find frightening parallels.

Prior to 1987, the main illegal drug used by black communities in the UK was cannabis. At that time, the stereotype among professionals in the drugs field, in the caring professions and, indeed, among the wider public was that black people generally were pro-cannabis. This stereotype had developed from a number of different roots: the use of cannabis in the 1950s by jazz musicians, many of whom were black; the use of cannabis by some members of the Jamaican community who arrived in the UK in the 1950s and 1960s; and the treatment of ganja as a 'holy herb' by Rastafarians. These images became translated as 'black people smoke dope'.

While it is undoubtedly true that cannabis was initially reintroduced into the UK from the Caribbean during this period, it is far from true to say that the drug was universally accepted even by Caribbean blacks. Many black people came to the UK with strong Christian traditions of evangelism or Catholicism, and were deeply disapproving of cannabis use. Those who did accept cannabis viewed it not as a drug, but as part of social culture. Its use was moderated foremost by social convention and showed no signs of being a major problem, either for black communities or for the wider community, until it was taken up by whites following the arrival in the 1960s of a drug culture involving many other drugs as well, initiated by drug use among the stars of popular music. While it could be said that the growth of a white youth market for cannabis stimulated a growth in supply-side activity among black individuals for a brief time, it was not long before the cannabis trade for white youth became dominated by white supply infrastructures.

The use of drugs other than cannabis was, until 1987, almost non-existent. Drugs such as speed, LSD and heroin were seen as 'chemical' as opposed to 'natural', and strong social and cultural norms limited their use, even among black youth, to all but a very few individuals. This was despite their poverty and high rates of unemployment.

What was going on in the black community throughout the 1970s and early 1980s was an upsurge in social awareness. This fight against social injustice, led in the main by young black men, had resulted in social unrest. Demonstrations and riots in Brixton, on Broadwater Farm, in Toxteth and among many other poor black communities were giving the authorities major cause for concern. Reports such as that by Lord Scarman were beginning to force British society to address issues such as racism and policing, and discrimination in employment.

Now if you are a conspiracy theorist, events from 1987 onwards take a sinister turn. If you believe that economics and racism are familiar bedfellows then your interpretation will be different, but still depressing. When Mr Stuttman from the Drug Enforcement Agency addressed UK drugs workers about crack (see Chapter 6), he was keen to stress that it was 'an equal opportunities drug'. But that part of his message was soon forgotten. Right from the start, crack was portrayed in the UK as a black drug, and its associations with violence conjured up images reminiscent of the Anslinger days in the USA. 'Crack equals black' images were everywhere. News reports showed us black crack dealers on the streets.

A black problem?

Hollywood gave us a series of films revolving around black gangs, black gangsters and crack. But it was not just the media who contributed to these associations. At NDAP, because of our early contact with the drug, we were constantly giving briefings to the Home Office and the Metropolitan Police about the nature of the drug and the main features of its impact. We were at great pains to stress that most of the crack users we were seeing were white, but it soon became clear that there was an implacable resistance to accepting this fact. We saw, for instance, a police briefing to help officers identify 'yardies', who were held to be responsible for most of the crack dealing in the UK. The description of a yardie as a well-dressed, polite black male of Jamaican origin driving an expensive German car could only result in one thing for black men: hassle from the police. We were just supposed to be getting away from stop and search (interestingly, since reintroduced on the back of the 'war on drugs'), and here was a new stereotype legitimizing a view of black males as automatically suspicious. We know also that research into local drug problems which identified crack use as a mainly white drug scene had the relevant paragraphs deleted. Officialdom did not want to hear the truth, for whatever reason.

Now I am not saying that crack use was non-existent within black communities. Indeed, crack found a niche early on that other drugs such as LSD and heroin had failed to find. There is no doubt that crack was marketed to young black males. We certainly had a case of nature imitating art. Black gangsters' movies and gangster rap have created an image of black males gaining wealth and power by selling crack and being ruthlessly violent, and they sold this image to everyone, including black youth, for whom it had a more urgent appeal. Here was a way for those at the bottom of the socio-economoic ladder to gain instant respect, instant access to the world that money could buy; here was the way out. The idea that you could make big money from selling crack increasingly led young black men into dealing, and gradually the fight against social injustice fell by the wayside.

This art–nature relationship became an ongoing dynamic. News and documentary coverage of crack focused almost exclusively on black dealers and users; we can only find two examples of British TV coverage of crack since 1989 that have shown white people involved. It could be argued that this came about because television and photographers need visual images and will therefore concentrate on the more easily visible side of the drugs trade, namely street dealing.

Those who are lowest on the socioeconomic scale will always be those who operate the lowest levels of dealing: on the streets as retail outlets for passing trade, the trade of those who have no access to a steady source of supply via a regular 'house' dealer, the trade of those 'on search'. Any retailers must be readily visible to prospective customers and are therefore equally visible to the media. If they are black, they are even more visible. If the media are directed to areas where dealing is visible, it is young black males they are most likely to see.

It is much harder to get good pictures of the white man or woman dealing from a house, or the dealer operating in the dim light of the club dance floor. It is harder to get pictures of the call-girl or the taxi-driver selling drugs. It is almost impossible to get good pictures of the transactions higher up the chain, of the wholesalers doing business. There are no newsworthy pictures of the financing of drug deals or of the many laundering operations, so the coverage was of young black males selling on the streets. The image was of the 'yardie' in expensive clothes, wearing gold chains, mobile phone in hand, driving a BMW with 'easy' women draped over the passenger seats, packing an uzi ready to blow away rivals. The whole community, including black people, was conditioned to believe that crack was a black drug.

In the years following the arrival of crack in 1987, political unrest in black communities withered away and crack use grew. Black dealers were not just selling to whites in passing trade. Increasingly, they began to deal within their own areas to black buyers.

There is no drugs economy in black communities. Crack is the big lie. Crack is a true product of the 1980s, packaged for speed, ease of use, quick turnover, instant personality-wrenching high, glitz and glamour and surface gloss, full of promises on which it singularly fails to deliver, all style no substance. The profits from its sale are not invested back in the community. The lion's share of the profits go to those who control the supply and distribution of the drug, to those who finance the deals. These people are white. Such capital does not exist among blacks. All they have to show is a few cars, mobile phones and pieces of jewellery.

What they have lost is of greater value

The black street dealing scene is contained within a few notorious areas where, to all intents and purposes, it is left alone for much of the time, except for the occasional high-profile operation involving hundreds of police, helicopters, dogs and the like. Areas such as Broadwater Farm in Tottenham, Granby Street and Toxteth in Liverpool, and St Paul's in Bristol have a 24–7–365 street scene, but are still deprived areas. Some might view this as a policy of containment: better to know where it is, to monitor it, to follow the drugs trail back up to the big-timers, than to disperse it into a hundred small, invisible pockets. But of course, while you know where it is, so do generations of prospective new customers, including young people.

On the other hand, some might view it as a deliberate and calculated policy of internalization, of chemical warfare, of controlled destruction of dissent. It is certainly true that economic conditions in these areas have not improved, that political awareness has largely disintegrated and that black youth now has a serious drug problem and a growing problem of gangsterism. Large-scale police operations in black areas are now under the banner of tackling drug dealing, not handling social unrest.

The challenge

The challenge for black communities themselves has been how to respond. The initial response was denial – understandably, considering the very real fears of the results of stereotyping and institutionalized racism. While the problem was only beginning this was almost justifiable.

The problem with denial is that it works internally as well as externally and leads to inaction. And the result of inaction is that the original problem grows unchecked. There can be many arguments about what might have been, had political leaders and organizations in black communities addressed the issues of alienated youth and crack head on, but attention was focused on the threat from outside. The question that is left open now is: how do we tackle crack?

Mainstream drugs services have not proved effective in addressing the problems of black drug users. There are many reasons for this, including the nature of treatment packages used – about which, more later. As we saw in Chapter 6, HIV-led funding in the late 1980s and early 1990s skewed services to focus on heroin and intravenous use, neither of which was a main feature of black drug use. There was a lack of black drug workers in the services, and a resulting failure of existing services to understand the history, politics and sensitivities of the drugs issue for black communities. In addition, drugs workers had themselves been arguing that crack was not going to be a problem. Finally, white drugs workers themselves had been conditioned to the same images of black drug use and gangsterism as everybody else. Workers were consequently scared of black users and crack, with its associations with violence. The result was yet more denial of the problem by those services which were meant to be there to help.

Early moves to develop services targeting black people were dogged by the prejudices of others. They were marginalized and demonized. They were labelled as radical and anti-white. Those working to develop the services were themselves often viewed as fundamentalists. This is not conjecture; we have had enough experience with NDAP to know this for fact. Even within our organization, which has a black director and supports the Black Drugs Workers' Forum, the struggle to create effective services for non-white users has not been painless. Even to raise the issue of race and drugs brings out concealed guilt and fear, and can be seen as divisive. But the reality remains that it is impossible to address the issue of drugs in the black community without looking at racism. We should not be afraid of this, seeing it as something that will tear us all apart. Rather we should see it as an opportunity, as a way of providing services that will bring us all, black and white, to a greater understanding.

Opening a Pandora's box

If there is no struggle there is no progress.
Those who profess to favour freedom and yet deprecate
    agitation ...
want crops without the thunder and lightening.
They want the ocean without the awful roar of its many
    waters. (Fanon)

The results of the devastation of black cultural identity are still with us every day. The bogeyman is a black man. Our language is still full of 'black equals bad, white equals good'. By and large, white people don't want to look at these issues because of a sense of guilt or fear of the envisaged repercussions. Similarly, many black people seek desperately for something to help them deny their experience. For many the answer is to try to be white, to gain an identity by taking on the trappings of white identity as represented by material success. Professional success will probably mean giving up most outward evidence of blackness save skin colour, and will almost certainly mean not rocking the boat by bringing up awkward issues of race. For those to whom professional success is denied, there has to be another way of filling the emptiness.

The easy answer, now that the political agitation has gone, is drug use. It is an accepted fact to anyone working in the caring professions that many abused people will turn to substance use to deny their experience. For black people, the abuse goes back for centuries and is part of their inheritance. Just as you cannot deal with the solvent user without dealing with the abuse, so you cannot deal with black drug use without dealing with the problem of identity, and this means addressing the issues of slavery and racism.

For those working with black drug users, this presents problems. First, if the drugs workers are white, can they understand the issues; do they know enough of the black experience of history and society? Second, regardless of who they are, are they in danger of releasing destructive forces within an individual? As Grier and Cobbs put it, in their book *Black Rage*:

> As grief lifts and the sufferer moves towards health, the hatred he had turned on himself is redirected toward his tormentors, and the fury of his attack on the one who caused him pain is in direct proportion to the depth of his grief ... Observe that the amount of rage the oppressed turns on his tormentor is a direct function of the depth of his grief, and consider the intensity of black men's grief.

At the moment, drug dealing and 'turf wars' have turned the anger within black people towards other black people. With no historical consciousness, all one black male sees when he faces another is himself. He has no respect for self, only a self-hatred that comes from being constantly told that he is not as good as white people. Therefore he has no problem in turning that hate on his psychological mirror image. Alternatively, the anger may remain as self-hatred and be masked by drug use, possibly of the kind which is carelessly self-destructive because the self is not seen as worthy of care. Of course, crack use can, as we have seen, actually promote delusions of grandeur, paranoia and violence, exacerbating the problem. The violence is then frequently directed at other black people, often female partners, and the quality and nature of family and child bearing become seriously damaged. If black drug users are to be helped away from their use, the self-hatred must be tackled and the issue of where all that anger will be directed must be addressed.

It is a legitimate anger, but it is equally clear that the role of the drugs worker is not to turn the user into an ex-user who attacks white people. Counselling therefore has to be capable of channelling that anger into non-destructive forms. Understanding must move beyond anger against oppressors identified by the colour of their skin – all white people – and towards an understanding of power structures. It is not some evil inherent in white people which made and makes many of them complicit in racism, but a complex political and economic situation in which many white people themselves are victims, although to a lesser extent. Counselling should move us to an understanding of self and through that to an understanding of others, to a commonality at its deepest level in our needs and motivations. This is not to pretend that the anger is somehow going to disappear, but to acknowledge that it is at racist situations and structures, and the mindset that created them, that it needs to be directed.

Whose therapy?

The very notion that existing methods of western counselling are appropriate to black drug users is, at best, questionable. Many of the concepts of the early psychotherapists were gained from Africa. It was following a visit to Africa that Jung came out with many of his ideas on symbolism, the collective unconscious, the spirit world, astral travel, numerology and the unseen and unheard. These ideas come from the mainstream of traditional African experience. Spirituality is as much a real part of existence in African culture as the material world.

The problem is that Jung brought back concepts that couldn't meet the demands of the dominant twentieth-century western mode of belief and verification: namely, science and scientific proof. They couldn't be measured and quantified, and as a result they became faulted and skewed by absorbing only the concepts that weren't too outrageous for European models of thought. This is a root of modern counselling, in a bastardized version of the aural hearing traditions of Africa. As a result, mainstream services can be seen as dealing with only part of an individual's problem, even if it deals with their history.

To take the theme further, if we look at 'alternative' therapies, which have become fashionable in work with crack users and whose benefits were referred to in Chapter 6, it is equally the case that we may be missing much of their therapeutic efficacy because we've only bought part of the package. Acupuncture, for instance, is a physical tool which in the East is part of a whole belief system. But we take the bit we want and totally disregard the rest, just as we take the cocaine away from the context of the coca leaf. Aromatherapy and reflexology are likewise manifestations of belief systems. Scientifically speaking, none of these practices should work, yet we know that they have practical effect, so science grudgingly accepts those aspects of belief systems whose effects can be measured and dismisses the concepts from which they grew.

The African and eastern traditions are based on holistic concepts which take into account all aspects of a person's existence, including faith and spirituality. The western scientific method, on the other hand, seeks answers by breaking down systems into component parts. For example, body and mind have long formed a dualism, resulting in western theories of psychological and physical addiction. Triage, the mechanism for the assessment of drug users recognized in the UK, deals with an individual's social situation, criminal behaviour and status, and physical and mental health. There is no room for soul or spirit. Yet in African cultures, spiritual well-being affects physical well-being; belief governs outcome (we have evidence for this through the use of placebo drugs) and the power of the mind is harnessed in recovery.

This is not to say that western science is wrong and African holistic beliefs are right. Scientific method clearly has a major role to play in both understanding and treatment. However, it should not play an exclusive role, and to dismiss other medicinal practices and belief systems is to display an arrogance that smacks of conceptual imperialism. Moreover, an individual's own beliefs, culture and world view are the ones the counsellor should work with, not the counsellor's.

I am not saying that drug use among black people is a problem caused by white people, which can't be solved because white people don't provide the right treatment packages – and that therefore all that can come out of this is guilt, hatred, doom and destruction. Afro-centrism says quite clearly that, just as an individual exists in the fullness of their experience of life on every level, so that individual is part of an extended community. What you do impacts upon your community, and you therefore have a responsibility to your community. While any services for black drug users need the support of the mainstream, the main impetus for developing responses to black drug use, and for developing services responsive to black drug users' needs, must come from the black communities themselves. It is only by black communities taking the lead that services can be developed that are truly centric to the needs of their clients.

On a practical level, what does this mean? First, it means that core services must reach out into the community via 'gateway' services. These 'gateway' services might be any local agencies or organizations, cultural, religious or otherwise, which present a face with which the user can identify: in other words, they must be of the community. Within these services, individuals need training, tailored to their needs and roles and beliefs, which will enable them to act as funnels or conduits, drawing and encouraging users towards more specialist drug service provision. This drug service provision must be ethnocentric in nature – not a black service, or a

Muslim service, or a Somali-specific service, but a service which can offer support that is centric to the user.

For the Muslim, it has to understand and acknowledge Islam in its working practice. For the Irishman or woman, it has to be able to understand and work with the experience of being Irish, to understand and acknowledge the impact of Catholicism and history upon an individual. For the Somali, it has to be able to offer drugs information that is not just translated from English into Somali, but which is translated to fit the *experience* of being Somali. In the end, the lessons which come from the development of drugs services and responses to drug use in the black community may prove essential to us all – in particular to other groups who have suffered oppression and discrimination, such as lesbians and people living with disabilities, but also to all of us in the drugs field or who use drugs.

8

Cold turkey

In almost every sense, the continued use of heroin represents the failure of the 'war on drugs'. What is more, it is likely to prove ultimately resistant to the policy 'Tackling Drugs Together' and any of its successors. The nature of the drug and its effects, and the histories and motivations of those who use it, form a potent force. The relative comfort with which its users can be handled by drugs workers without their actually having to, or being able to, get many users to a state of abstinence compounds the problem. Heroin policy and treatment are in danger of slipping into their own narcotic dream-like state, and unless someone discovers some new wonder-drug alternative treatment, they are unlikely to wake up in the near future.

The so-called 'British system' for dealing with heroin users – namely, certain doctors being able to prescribe heroin to registered users – is dead. An experimental attempt to revive it under Dr John Marks in the north-west of England was ended after a few years of trial for a number of reasons, the main one being its cost. The standard treatment for heroin use in the UK today is the prescription of oral methadone. While there is no doubt that – together with needle exchanges and the promotion of safer injecting and safer sex – this type of treatment helps greatly to reduce the risk and spread of HIV, there is little sign of it being effective in stopping people from using heroin.

Increasing restrictions, policing and penalties have not stopped the flow of heroin. Since the 1960s, heroin use seems to have followed an inevitable pattern: the number of users surges upwards for three or four years, then stabilizes, then surges up again. The one thing it doesn't do is go down. Following the last surge in use in the early 1980s, when smokeable-grade heroin arrived in quantity from the Middle East, we now seem to be seeing the signs of another upturn.

Welcome to the pleasure dome

What is it about opiates that has made them a feature of both recreation and medicine for thousands of years, despite public censure and moral disapproval? What is it about them that has caused wars to be fought and international regulation to be introduced? Why, with all this experience, have we not been able to get on top of the opiate problem?

The powers of the opium poppy have been known for thousands of years, certainly since Sumerian civilization in 4000 BC. It has been used since that time for both medicinal and hedonistic purposes. The Ancient Greeks saw opium as a substance which could drown cares, treat many ailments and produce dreams which physicians could analyse as part of their assessment of patients. Opium's addictive properties were also well known right from these earliest records. In pill form, as laudanum, opium was used in western medicine from the early 1500s, became as easy to obtain by the mid-1800s as aspirin is today – being the active ingredient in a plethora of pills and potions – and was not restricted until 1908. By the mid-1800s, morphine has been synthesized from opium and competed with it on the pharmacists' shelves; morphine was initially seen as a cleaner (it was injectable) and less addictive alternative to opium.

The hedonistic use of opium centres on the twilight world it creates in the user: it places the user in a state somewhere between being awake and asleep, and creates dreams of amazing complexity and detail. To understand this state more completely, the curious should read Thomas De Quincey's *Confessions of an English Opium Eater* or several of the works of Coleridge, the most famous being his poem 'Kubla Khan'. It is probably the use of opium by the Victorian romantics as a creative tool that led many artists, writers and particularly musicians to turn to opiate drugs for inspiration. But opiates, particularly the more powerful compounds such as morphine and heroin, flatter to deceive.

Heroin is active through its biotransformation into morphine, but is around three times as potent as morphine. It penetrates the blood–brain barrier faster, and when it reaches the brain each heroin molecule is broken down to become morphine molecules. Heroin can be smoked, snorted, dabbed, swallowed or injected, the main difference between methods being the speed of effect – smoking and injecting are the most rapid.

Morphine reaches all body tissues. One-third attaches to blood proteins and the rest accumulates in the kidney, liver, lungs and spleen. Its effects last for around four or five hours, with 90 per cent being metabolized and excreted within 24 hours. As a psychoactive substance, it is particularly alluring because it is active on systems which have receptors ready and waiting for it.

The body has its own natural opiate painkiller called beta-endorphin, a neuropeptide, which is produced in the brain and the pituitary gland. These neuropeptides produce the natural analgesia which causes obliviousness to pain following terrible injuries, and imperviousness to pain in religious trance states. They act as naturally occurring opiate pathways with specific receptor sites.

The major effects of morphine are in the central nervous system, where it causes euphoria and analgesia, and in the gastrointestinal tract, where it causes constipation. As narcotics, one would expect the opiates to induce sleep, but this is not the full picture. Although heavy-eyed 'nodding' or 'gauching out' is a common sight among opiate users, it is in fact the 'twilight zone', not sleep, that is being entered. Any actual sleep is very light, but is rich in dreams. Such euphoria is an initial attraction of drugs like heroin, but is one of the first sensations to diminish with continued heavy use. People dependent on heroin for a long period are usually more concerned with getting enough of the drug to 'stay level' than with getting a major 'hit'.

One of the initial discouragements from heroin use is the likelihood of vomiting. Morphine stimulates areas of the brain that cause nausea, and directly induces contractions in the upper gastrointestinal tract, causing vomiting. This effect is quite common with initial use, but for most users it wears off with repeated use. As a result, many people never go beyond their first hit of heroin, seeing this particular side effect as too unpleasant to repeat. Others, however, see vomiting as of no importance compared to the intense euphoric state.

The other effect of morphine on the gastrointestinal tract is to interfere with movement of food through the bowel and to inhibit the entry of digestive juices. The resulting dry, slow-moving faecal matter then has more water removed, causing hardening and still slower movement. Morphine then tightens the anal muscle and distracts the user from internal warnings that it is time to defecate. Even for long-term heroin users, constipation is a constant problem.

Morphine also suppresses the 'cough centre' of the brain, hence the use of another opium derivative, codeine, as an ingredient of cough medicines. It also depresses pituitary functions, which may cause an initial increase in testosterone levels in the blood and a correspondingly decreased sex drive, but tolerance to this effect generally develops. The main effect on sexuality seems to be to decrease the importance of sexual desires compared to the other pleasures of the drug, resulting not in impotence but in less sexual obsession.

Another sensation produced by morphine is a warm, flushed feeling resulting from the drug causing blood vessels in the skin to dilate. This, combined with the analgesia, creates the sensation of womb-like warmth and well-being which is so desired by most heroin users.

In fact, the attraction of this 'feeling' is heightened by the particular way in which morphine has its analgesic effect. While morphine undoubtedly does affect the pathways carrying messages of pain from affected areas of the body to the brain, it is on 'suffering' – the user's emotional reactions, expectations and memory of previous experiences of pain – that it has its most marked effect. In other words, the user might feel pain but not experience the suffering that goes with it: the pain seems of no consequence. This effect seems to operate not only on physical pain, but also on emotional pain, having the effect of making traumatic experiences in the user's life seem unimportant. In the womb of heroin, all unpleasantness can be temporarily forgotten. It is therefore the ideal drug of escape. Why face up to problems created by, say, sexual abuse during childhood, when you can just make them unimportant? One common difficulty for long-term users coming off heroin is the re-emergence of long-ignored emotional and psychological traumas, which then have to be faced up to and dealt with differently. It is much easier to run away again.

A significant side effect of morphine on the central nervous system is respiratory depression. Breathing becomes slow, irregular and shallow. Morphine also deadens the brain's response to increasing levels of carbon dioxide in the blood, which is the body's warning of the need to breathe faster and take in more oxygen. This respiratory depression is what kills people who overdose. Given that the purity level of street heroin is unpredictable, it is easy to misjudge the quantity of intake and so overdose.

This is a particular problem for those who have come off heroin and then relapsed. The body's tolerance to the drug may have decreased, and their old level of intake may easily now be an overdose.

The attractions of heroin can be readily seen. It induces a warm, euphoric, dream-like state in which physical and emotional pain seem of little note. It is a drug on which you can continue to function: there is no sensory impairment. Maybe you will be the one who can carry out the balancing act, keeping intake regulated to levels and frequencies which avoid the onset of dependency. Yes, it is a risky drug, but doesn't that add to its status? And besides, when you're gauching, who cares about the risks? Nothing can touch you. The only thing to worry about is withdrawal.

Withdrawal, the signs of physical dependence, have assumed a mythical enormity in heroin lore. Many heroin users identify their first signs of withdrawal both as a 'badge' denoting their habit and as something to be feared and avoided at all costs because of the terror they hold. The danger is that avoiding withdrawal symptoms can become such an overriding aim that they are seen as the main focus of treatment for those seeking help, to the detriment of looking at the main reasons for dependence, which are, as with all other drugs, wrapped up in the function that the drug plays in the user's life. Unless that function is replaced by an alternative – and here I do not mean another drug – then abstinence becomes an almost impossible goal.

Withdrawal without medication is undoubtedly extremely unpleasant. For between four and seven days after cessation, the habitual user will have the symptoms of severe flu. As Newton said, 'For every action there is an equal and opposite reaction', and this perfectly describes drug 'comedowns'. The effects that heroin has in depressing body functions and pain are replaced by a kind of opposite sensation as systems begin to re-establish themselves towards equilibrium. Common withdrawal symptoms include gooseflesh, hot and cold flushes, sweating, runny nose, weeping eyes, aching muscles and joints, restlessness, insomnia, anxiety, nightmares, stomach cramps, vomiting, diarrhoea, panting breath, weakness and irritability. It is easy, however, to medicate against withdrawal. The problem is that the drug most commonly prescribed to deal with withdrawal symptoms, methadone, itself has a number of major drawbacks.

A major factor of withdrawal that cannot be overlooked is 'craving', just as with cocaine. Even with long-term methadone reduction programmes, when the methadone dosage gets to low levels it is common for the craving for heroin to return. Treatment programmes for heroin therefore have to incorporate all the mechanisms for dealing with craving that we referred to in Chapter 6 when looking at 'crack'. Similarly, the feelings of grief at the loss of the state of euphoria have to be addressed as with any dependency.

Just another addiction?

Methadone reduction programmes have become the norm in the UK for treatment of heroin dependency. There are many attractions in this type of response for treatment agencies. Methadone, although not chemically similar to morphine, binds to the same receptor sites. It is a good analgesic, but has a much weaker euphoriant effect. It is absorbed well orally, which helps agencies to move the user away from injecting and its attendant risks. About 90 per cent of an intake of methadone binds in blood tissues and some binds in the brain. It has a longer-lasting effect than heroin, about a day to a day and a half, so the dose doesn't have to be repeated as often. Furthermore, by comparison to heroin, its withdrawal symptoms are mild.

However, methadone has problems as a treatment. First, it is itself addictive and many would argue against the morality of substituting one dependency for another. For agencies, paradoxically, there is also an advantage because clients will be more likely to represent just in order to collect their prescription. This may look good in the statistics, but is it effective? It is certainly true that the agency that decided not to provide methadone would be taking a very brave step, as client numbers would almost certainly collapse. Beside the moral argument, the fact is that there are many more overdose deaths from methadone than heroin. Are we not, therefore, substituting one dangerous drug with another that is even more dangerous?

The aim with methadone is to reduce dependency on street drugs, to draw users into contact with agencies, to reduce the risk of HIV infection and to reduce levels of crime. In most of these aims, methadone can claim success. However, there is an illegal market in methadone, users commonly 'top up' their prescription by using heroin in order to get the desired euphoria, and over the course of a long-term reduction programme it is easy for even the well motivated to forget that it is abstinence towards which they are working.

Then we have the problem of the return of heroin craving at low dosages. Heroin users, by and large, don't enjoy methadone, not just because it gives them a less euphoriant effect, but because (unlike heroin, which allows the user's brain a fair degree of active clarity at least at low dosages) it fogs the mind, creating in some a zombie-like state. Physicians like Dr John Marks argue that it is no more morally repugnant to prescribe diamorphine (heroin) on maintenance doses than methadone, and that this would remove entirely the need for street heroin, illegal markets and drug-related acquisitive crime. However, this approach has been rejected for financial reasons and, one suspects, because it would be difficult for any government to obtain approval for prescribing a drug that actually got people 'high'. We don't like the pleasure principle, do we?

More important than drugs

Methadone had in any case been 'locked' into treatment programmes by the 1988 report by the Advisory Council on the Misuse of Drugs. *Aids and Drug Misuse Part 1* stated that 'HIV is a greater danger to individual and public health than drug misuse. Accordingly, we believe that services which aim to minimise HIV risk behaviour by all available means should take precedence in development plans.'

The aim was for a range of community-based projects to provide a range of services aimed at keeping users in contact with agencies and away from practices that might spread HIV. While on one level this can be seen as a positive step, introducing more user-friendly services and legitimizing harm reduction such as needle exchanges and free condoms, it also caused major problems. As stated in Chapter 6, all UK drug budgets were allocated from HIV funds in District and Regional Health Authorities. Most of the bureaucrats in charge of these budgets were recruited from gay and lesbian ranks in a clear attempt by health authorities to build in an understanding of what, at the time, was still seen as a problem mainly among gay males in the UK and to avoid labelling and insensitivity.

Unfortunately, many of those who thus had their hands on the purse strings were strong on sexuality and sexual health, but weak on drug use and drug services. If you weren't working with intravenous users (and thus mainly with heroin users), there was no funding for you. Work on other drugs – and users generally come to heroin via other drugs – was virtually eliminated for a time. A new political correctness arrived with the focus on HIV, to be layered on top of the 'hip cool' of the already liberal drugs field. Orthodoxies were established which were seen as unchallengeable.

One of these was methadone maintenance, formally described as more flexible and responsive prescribing.

By the early 1990s, the huge HIV budgets were suddenly gone. For a while, more had been spent on drugs than on any disease in the history of medicine. And the expected heterosexual epidemic had not occurred to anywhere near the levels predicted in the gloom-and-doom warnings of the AIDS 'industry' in the mid-1980s. HIV could now be more readily marginalized again as an issue for 'unpopular' groups such as gay men and drug users. The media had moved on and the new threats were first crack and then ecstasy. The emphasis of government drugs policy shifted once again, this time towards 'community safety' and drug-related crime.

Now all of these issues are actually important. Drugs agencies need to develop strategies and services dealing with all these problems. However, if we are plunged from a total focus on one issue to the detriment of all others such as with HIV, and then suddenly all of our attention has to switch to another, we set ourselves up to fail. This is especially true when the funding follows the latest media-led 'priority'. In fairness, the policy 'Tackling Drugs Together' does attempt to strike some sort of balance. The liberal language of the harm reduction approach heralded by the Advisory Council on the Misuse of Drugs has gone, and abstinence is once again the clear thrust of policy. Fortunately, while the language might be gone, the main planks of harm reduction as part of a range of strategies are clearly here to stay; in this respect, we are certainly not back to the attitudes of the early 1980s 'war on drugs'.

Intravenous use does throw up a particular range of problems for drug users, and these have to be addressed. It is a favoured method among heroin users because all the drug is seen as 'getting there', unlike smoking where some of the expensive drug smoulders away between 'pulls'. Furthermore, it offers a 'rush' as the drug gets quickly to the brain. Safer injecting advice is not just to do with the transmission of HIV or hepatitis, although not sharing remains a major priority, as does teaching those who do occasionally share how to clean needles and syringes first (many, however, cannot wait for a lengthy cleaning process to be completed between seeing their friend or partner have a 'hit' and having their own). Injecting can cause many other major problems. As a vein is repeatedly injected into, scar tissue forms and some veins collapse, causing circulation problems. It is hard to inject as each area becomes too damaged to use. Unclean injecting equipment or an unclean injecting site can cause infection, creating sores and abscesses. Impurities in street heroin or lumps of solid matter left when tablets are crushed up for injection can block or cause damage to veins. Hitting an artery by mistake is not only painful, but can cause major damage, leading to amputation or death.

Despite these dangers, users will continue to inject. We have worked with users who have injected into veins through abscesses, and who continue to share despite a full knowledge of the risks. While it is true that such behaviour appears not only sordid but also recklessly self-destructive, it is important to understand that, psychological reasons apart, once that rush comes on such considerations become totally unimportant to the user because that is the effect of the drug.

Education of the heroin user remains important even if it is sometimes less than effective. Beyond injecting advice there is the issue of drug combinations. Few users are purists. Many heroin users are walking encyclopaedias of opiate drugs, knowing at least as much about heroin substitutes or enhancers as pharmacists. These alternatives include artificial opiates such as pethidine, palfium, diconal, dihydrocodeine, fortral, temgesic and methadone itself, as well as other legal and illegal drugs. For many, alas, such knowledge is dangerously inaccurate or incomplete, and needs to be completed.

Once again, though, the message is that such education needs to be on the terms of the user if it is to be understood and acted upon. Mass media campaigns on heroin have notoriously missed the mark, including the billboards warning against sharing and HIV. Admen seem instinctively to go for 'shock/horror' imagery where heroin is involved – individuals deteriorating in health and appearance over a few frames of film; giant needles and blood; dire warnings of consequences. Perhaps this is because that is all they see of the subject they are dealing with, or perhaps the advertisements are aimed more at the general public than the user (see, we're doing something!). Whatever the case, such imagery holds no fear for heroin users. They do not feel the same squeamishness about needles as some others do. A deteriorating self-image is not an issue. The drug takes care of such concerns.

Effective education has been provided by a few agencies, notably the 'Grandpa Smackhead Jones' comics produced by Lifeline Manchester, but once again it is a controversial issue. Such approaches were more acceptable in the non-judgmental years of HIV harm reduction. We are now into community safety and abstinence, and it remains to be seen whether approaches such as 'Grandpa Jones' will not soon be attacked by the media as 'condoning' drug use.

Mixed messages

The decision about whether we are reducing harm, legitimizing or punishing lies at the heart of the problem of responding to heroin use. In the early 1980s we were fighting it, aiming for abstinence, no matter what, and punishing. By the late 1980s we were reducing harm, being non-judgmental. Now we're edging back to punishing. These swings can cause major problems for services, but they are there because we have, ultimately, no answer that works. If we legalized heroin, we would have less acquisitive crime and users would not need to share needles or inject impurities into their systems, but with a drug as addictive as heroin, we would end up with many more users and users with dependencies. If we go all out for punishment and abstinence, we encourage the growth of organized crime, the spread of HIV (because we could drive the problem further underground and away from services) and deaths from secondary health problems. If we go for non-judgmental harm reduction while the drug remains illegal, the health and legal issues will continue to contradict themselves, often dangerously. This is seen most clearly at present in the prison system.

Prisons in the UK have long been known to be rife with drug use. Most injecting drug users will expect to spend some of their life in prison, either for possession and supply or for the crimes they commit to support their habit. To this can be added large numbers of inmates who use other drugs either recreationally or through a habit. This represents a major challenge for the prison service because it throws measures aimed at punishment and those aimed at tackling health issues into stark opposition.

The supply of drugs in prisons undoubtedly adds to levels of violence and intimidation. Now it is not the 'tobacco barons' who hold sway, it is the drug suppliers. On the other hand, the use of drugs with a sedative effect, such as cannabis and, to an extent, heroin, can also have a calming effect on the behaviour of those who use them. Attempts to halt the supply of drugs to inmates have at best been disruptive.

Those bringing in drugs as visitors are arrested on a daily basis, but supplies still get through. Perversely, many of those so arrested themselves end up in custody, so increasing the demand on the inside. In response to this problem, the Home Office has introduced a system of random drug testing for inmates, targeting 60,000 prisoners each year.

On the surface this appears to be an eminently practical way of tackling the problem, but it actually creates major problems. The penalties for a positive test or for refusing a test are a further 28 days on sentence, confinement to cells and a loss of privileges and earnings – certainly enough to make being caught a thing to be avoided. For individuals with a heroin habit, however, giving up can be a long and painful process, particularly if they are not to relapse, and for some giving up straight away is not something that can be done alone and without the necessary support. Such individuals will continue to use – after all, the likelihood of prison in the first place was no deterrent.

Heroin is also relatively quick to leave the system and, for the user without an established habit, therefore presents a relatively good option for avoiding detection in random tests. Cannabis, on the other hand, stays detectable in the body for weeks and presents a strong likelihood of being caught. It would therefore seem likely that cannabis users will switch to substances that offer less possibility of detection. So measures designed to cut down drug use may, perversely, actually increase the use of injectable drugs. Violence and intimidation around the supply of an expensive, scarce and 'must have' drug like heroin are likely to be higher than those around a cheaper, more easily available and more 'take it or leave it' substance like cannabis.

If prisons are to attempt, through testing and punishment, to stop the use of drugs, it follows that they must continue to prohibit the use and availability of injecting equipment. This means that injecting drug users in prison are far more likely to share needles and 'works'. It is not uncommon to find one old and worn needle and syringe being shared by a dozen intravenous drug users. The logic of deterrence also dictates that the strong bleach needed to clean works before use cannot be available, both because of its potential use as a weapon and because it would appear to condone the very activity the authorities are trying to eliminate.

The risks of prisoners contracting HIV and hepatitis are therefore enormously increased. This presents a threat not just to those prisoners, but to the community outside prisons. Those same drug users will leave prison and interact with others, either through sharing of 'works' or sexual activity. If they all followed safe injecting and safer sex practices, this would present no problem; but in reality, this will not always be the case. The prison service could thus be seen as a major factor in the transmission of HIV and hepatitis.

Let us add to these difficulties by looking at the effect of such deterrence on drug treatment. It is a well-established fact that the more a problem is 'policed', the more it is driven underground. If you require treatment for a drug habit, it is far less likely that you will actively seek that treatment in a climate of enforced prohibition; you will be inviting scrutiny and possible punishment.

The knock-on effect is that you will be more likely to leave prison with a habit or relapse into a previous habit upon release. Support networks will not have been established and the problem will have remained untackled during your sentence. Even were you to seek help, appropriate help is unlikely to be forthcoming. Prison doctors will not be, and are not, unaware of the climate which operates in their institution. Some prison doctors already refuse to prescribe methadone detoxification.

Outside prison, very few services will carry out methadone detox in less than seven weeks, and they have the whole range of support counselling and therapies at their disposal. An unsupported one-week detox programme is therefore very unlikely to prove effective, leaving those who arrive with a habit with the alternatives of going into withdrawal or taking the risk and continuing to use illegal supplies of heroin inside. The problem is that to provide adequate health care and treatment would be to acknowledge an ongoing problem of drug use in prisons. In reality, given the contribution of drug use to acquisitive crime, this is likely to be the situation for the foreseeable future; if it cannot be admitted, little is likely to be done that will have any effect.

Government guidelines call for treatment centres to make themselves more accessible and appropriate to prisons and prisoners' needs. This throws the onus back on to outside agencies, which are going not only to be given inadequate funds for such work, but also to lack clear guidelines and specifications for how treatment will operate. While there is some fine work already being undertaken in prisons by outside agencies, it remains to be seen how access to those with problems will be affected by a random testing regime.

There are two basic approaches to tackling drugs as a health issue in prisons. The first is to provide funding and systems for prison doctors to offer services inside which mirror those provided on the outside: non-judgmental and easy-access counselling and support, prescribing, clean injecting equipment and a proper system of drugs education (preferably provided on a 'peer' education model, using both ex and current prisoners in discussion groups and workshops), plus a clear system of 'pick-up' and aftercare when an individual leaves prison. For the reasons outlined above, we are unlikely to see such a system introduced. Making drug use in prison easier or more acceptable through a more relaxed regime may increase levels of usage.

The second option is to try to avoid users being sucked into the prison system in the first place. At present, if you have committed crimes to support a drug problem, it is a difficult decision as to whether to declare the drug use as a motivating factor in court. It may work against a custodial sentence or it may work for one; it depends on the knowledge and attitudes of the magistrate or judge, and this varies enormously from individual to individual. One thing is clear: those who receive treatment are far more likely to break the spiral of drug use and offending than those who go into prison. Indeed, many of the clients with whom we have worked actually got their drug habits in custody. Even were drugs not available inside, returning to the same environment and circumstances that existed before imprisonment is likely to lead to relapse and reoffending.

Keeping them out

The Department of Health's recent 'Effectiveness Review' has shown that treatment is more effective than custody. If someone can become drug free with ongoing support in their own community, they are much less likely to reoffend. Furthermore, treatment is a much less expensive option than prison. If the 12,000 injecting drug users who were in UK prisons in 1994 had been put into treatment instead, the savings would have been considerable. If the money saved were to be spent on treatment and education services, those services would be improved and the numbers offending as a result of drug use would hopefully decrease. If the assets seized from dealers by the courts were channelled into the funding of drugs services instead of being eaten up by the Treasury, matters could be improved still further.

So what about compulsory treatment as an alternative to custody? Many drugs agencies oppose such a compulsory system on the grounds that treatment cannot work if a client is not personally committed to it; if it is done under duress, true re-evaluation and real action on the part of clients will not take place. Much better results are gained with those who present at drugs services from an act of free will and a personal commitment to cease using drugs compared to those who are 'forced' by others or by circumstance. Many users attend under pressure from partners, family or friends, or because they have a custodial sentence, or because their drug use has affected their finances, housing situation or options in life so negatively that they have little other option. Choice in life's decisions is rarely truly free – outside pressures usually push individuals towards a certain course of action.

If this is true of drug-related offending, it is similarly true of decisions to attend treatment. Our agency has found through its work with young people that those who attend counselling because they have been 'caught' by parents or teachers are just as likely to benefit as those who have self-referred.

To summarize, if treatment can break the cycle of drug use and offending while at the same time reducing the spread of HIV and hepatitis, then the justice system should be adapted to provide for this. However, if drug users are to be placed in custody, it is difficult for the system to provide treatment packages which will achieve those outcomes. Instead it may introduce measures which attempt to avoid those in prisons continuing to break the law while inside.

Ultimately, again, such decisions are political and are taken in the light of media and social pressures. If someone has broken into your house and taken all your belongings, it is difficult to accept that they will not be punished for their actions, but instead will receive treatment while remaining in the community. Imagine the furore there would be in the press if such a system were to be introduced. The first accusation would be that, in order to avoid a prison sentence, burglars need only claim they had a drug problem. We would be accused of being 'soft on crime' as well as 'soft on drugs'. It would be a brave Home Secretary indeed who introduced such measures as a cornerstone of policy. Not only are the issues not clear cut, but they are also muddied by a lack of public understanding or informed debate, and by the fear of banner headlines.

Given the pattern of increase, levelling out and increase again in the number of heroin users, and given the drug's capacity to promote allegiance and habit, it would appear that heroin is giving us a clear message: the war on drugs has been lost and it's time for a change of policy. At £20,000 per kilo wholesale, converting to £300,000 per kilo street retail, there will never be a shortage of those prepared to take the risks involved in its supply. With users commonly spending £70 per day on the drug, the cost to society in acquisitive crime is estimated at around £1–2 billion per year. If policing pushes up the price of heroin, users have to steal more or prostitute themselves further to pay for the increase. If policing is ineffective and the price falls, more people can afford to get involved with the drug.

To legalize the drug would necessitate a price decrease of such magnitude that users would no longer need to steal to buy it, which in turn would mean that it was cheap enough and sufficiently available for anyone to get a habit. Decriminalizing possession while continuing to prosecute and pursue suppliers would continue the involvement of organized crime and keep prices and acquisitive crime high. It would also cut off many of the means available to the police for identifying and prosecuting dealers. On the other hand, it would undoubtedly cut the number of casualties among users. It has also been argued that it would shift the responsibility for dealing with drug users away from the police and make it primarily a health issue. However, users would still be dealt with by the police and the courts for acquisitive crime.

The real message that heroin sends us is that there is no easy solution to this problem. Whatever we do has benefits and negative consequences. This drug will not go away. The reality may be that we will always be dealing with compromise solutions and that the best we can do is keep the situation stable. After all, there must be a limit to the number of people who would use the drug, mustn't there? Unfortunately we might find ourselves in the situation of finding out the answer to that particular question.

9

Nothing is real

Lysergic acid diethylamide (LSD) is a drug of revelation, a drug that poses awkward questions. It certainly reveals a few interesting facts about the reasons why authority views some drugs as especially dangerous. LSD is the least addictive of all drugs and kills very few people indeed, and yet it is a class A drug under the UK Misuse of Drugs Act. It also poses questions about the degree of concern that authority shows for the well-being of its citizens, given the early US experiments with the drug, carried out on unwilling and often unwitting subjects. LSD is also a unique drug in that, at one time and for one generation, it was a drug whose disruption of all that had previously been taken for granted held out the promise (or threat) of changing the world. With the drug itself, that promise turned out to be an illusion.

It is certainly a drug whose impact on individual lives has been immense, not in the sense that it has dragged them down into addiction, but in so far as it has thrust them into a relative universe, where nothing is absolute, nothing is without question. For some, it has taken them on a journey which has left them with no way home. LSD is an unforgiving drug, razor sharp, a drug that can turn in 'Strawberry Fields', 'Lucy in the Sky with Diamonds', 'Purple Haze' and 'Mr Tambourine Man'. It is also the drug of Charles Manson.

LSD is an hallucinogen. The use of drugs for hallucinatory purposes goes back for thousands of years and crosses many different cultures. From the Greeks to the Aztecs, hallucinatory experience was regarded as information from a higher order of experience than day-to-day reality. It informed art and illustrated religion. Modern scientific reality discounts such experience. The visions of deities and angels of the past are today considered signs of insanity, but cultural context is everything; we have no context today by which to value such experiences. As a result, the rediscovery of hallucinatory substances and experiences by western culture in the 1950s and 1960s was like a cultural earthquake. We had no idea where to slot it and no utilitarian purpose for it (although, as we shall see, we tried to find one). In the end, it was in popular youth culture that hallucinogens became available, and artists and intellectuals like Aldous Huxley began to experiment with these in the 1950s. There is the fly agaric mushroom of children's books, mescaline from the peyote cactus, psilocybe mushrooms, morning glory seeds, and exotica such as bufotenine found in the glands of certain toads, but the drug that had the most dramatic impact on popular culture was LSD.

LSD derives from ergot, a fungus that infects a variety of grains, and which has a long history of producing hallucinations. Grain had its own goddess in ancient Greece – Demeter – and Plato, Aristotle and Socrates all took part in hallucinatory rituals in her name. Mostly, however, mouldy grain has affected people through the ages who had no intention of hallucinating, but had merely eaten infected grain or bread. Ergotism is unpleasant and often leads to death, and it may have been the cause of the medieval condition known as St Anthony's Fire, which, alongside gangrene, also caused hallucinations.

From plant to laboratory

Chemists have long been interested in ergot. In 1918 the Swiss chemist Dr Arthur Stoll isolated the first ergot alkaloid at the Sandoz laboratories. His work was taken up by another Sandoz chemist, Dr Albert Hoffman, who was exploring ergot alkaloids for possible applications in obstetrics, geriatrics and the treatment of migraine, and as a circulatory and respiratory stimulant. In 1938 he synthesized lysergic acid diethylamide 25, but it was not until an unfortunate accident in 1943 that he discovered the remarkable properties of the substance. Accidentally self-administering the drug, he found himself soon transported into a world of fantastic visions. A unique bike ride home and a visit from the doctor in an attempt to treat this 'nervous breakdown' ended in an exhausted sleep. The next day Hoffman awoke and found 'The world was as if newly created.'

In the following years, research into potential uses for this remarkable substance followed two courses, one of honourable intent and one of almost unbelievably underhanded amorality. The 'honourable' was the investigation of the drug for potential medical use, although the methodology used often showed an alarming lack of understanding of the intensity of the LSD experience. Subjects were often injected with high doses of the drug, rocketing them almost instantly to the peak of intense hallucinatory experience. The drug was explored for its effect on repressed memory in psychoanalysis; for the controlled study of psychosis; for the treatment of alcoholics; for the relief of pain; for the treatment of arthritis, skin rashes, paralysis and headaches. The results were often contradictory: the often beneficial effects were offset by suicides and psychoses. By the early 1960s, clinical research was effectively over, with no conclusively beneficial application having been discovered.

The other course followed by research was into 'military' applications. Here the research methods not only were often dubious, but also showed scant regard for morality. Experiments were carried out in the United States by the Army Chemical Corps, often on US troops who had no idea what to expect, into the drug's potential as an incapacitating agent for use against enemy soldiers. The army also explored its use as a means of reversing 'brainwashing'. The CIA investigated LSD use as a brainwashing agent and as an interrogational 'truth drug' (although the mind boggles at the kind of 'truths' that it would have revealed). CIA agents would administer the drug to servicemen and prisoners, and watch the results through two-way mirrors.

It would seem clear that the fight against communism was seen as bestowing on the authorities the right to experiment on their own citizens – without their consent or knowledge, and regardless of the danger to their life, limb or sanity – using a drug that was considered harmful enough to be made illegal a few short years later, even when used knowingly by private individuals. But a chemical explored for use in war soon became centre stage in another theatre of war – the 'war on drugs'.

LSD's potential as an incapacitating agent

And on to the street

The transition of LSD from medical and military research into widespread popular use was facilitated by the extolling of its virtues by key individuals and the expiry of the Sandoz patent in 1963, which allowed its legal manufacture by others.

The main evangelists of LSD were two Harvard University professors – Timothy Leary and Dr Richard Alpert – and a Stratford University student, later to turn author, Ken Kesey. Leary's experiments with LSD and other phsychedelic drugs quickly transformed him from a promising clinical psychologist into a character wearing white flowing robes and exhorting American youth to 'turn on, tune in and drop out'. The authorities could hardly fail to take notice of somebody carrying out such a strange but high-profile marketing campaign on behalf of a mind-altering chemical; this was, after all, pre-Beatles America and their experiments could hardly be presented as scientific.

The final straw was an article of Leary's in the *Journal of Atomic Scientists*, which suggested that the government should dose the water supply to prepare the public for a similar action by the Soviet enemy. Now, this was crazy talk: clearly the talk of someone whose grip of this world had loosened while his grip on other worlds became stronger. Any sane authorities would have ridiculed him rather than giving him credibility. But this was an America still recovering from the bizarre nightmares of the McCarthy era, where communist threats existed everywhere. This was already a world where almost any insanity was believable as a real threat if it could be presented as anti-American. The CIA was on to Leary. In May 1963 he was sacked from Harvard. This spurred him on to establish experimental communities dedicated to using LSD to achieve spiritual goals. In summer 1963 he and Alpert established the International Foundation for Internal Freedom.

For the next five years, LSD hysteria grew. Archetypally, there were those who argued that it represented an opportunity for humanity to leap to a higher plane, and those who saw it as burning the brains of the young and undermining society at its very foundations. Of course, in retrospect it was neither of these things. LSD was the right drug for its time. It fitted perfectly into the new youth culture – young people with disposable income, plenty of jobs available, new technology promising to unburden humans of the toil of this world by providing cheap and inexhaustible sources of energy, a world where anything seemed possible and the future was bright. Antibiotics promised an end to diseases which had plagued humans for thousands of years. Material goods and material values were no longer something that had to be striven for: for much of white western youth, the life of plenty was here and now.

Suddenly, the life of plenty was not enough. There had to be more to life and existence. Youth culture could campaign for a whole range of 'rights' and fairnesses, but it had also turned its eye to the spiritual. For much of western youth, traditional western religions were bankrupt. They had no answer for a Darwinian and Einsteinian universe where there were no absolutes, no absolute values. The graffiti of the time proclaimed 'God is dead' (or alternatively, 'Clapton is God'!). Eastern religions seemed to be more in tune with relativity, eternity and infinity, and to offer altered states of awareness in the here and now via meditation, rather than a promise of some unspecified reward after death.

LSD fitted this scenario perfectly. From 1963 to 1968 LSD use exploded and became widespread. Musicians, artists and then young people generally began to use the drug. Love-ins and festivals were fuelled by the psychedelic experience. Here was the instant route to nirvana. It is easy to see it now as a kind of spiritual equivalent to instant mashed potato – throwaway and ultimately lacking in nourishment; an illusion. By 1968 the drug had become a schedule 1 illegal substance, and by the early 1970s the dream was over, flower-power and hippies were gone, and drugs such as heroin and cocaine were taking over. Leary himself later recanted, appearing all along to have been what he later became: a stand-up philosopher and comic.

To talk to today's youth about LSD as a key to the doors of perception, a way of unlocking great secrets, is rather like trying to sell them visions of a perfect, poverty- and war-free world. Such talk has no meaning for them. For the young nowadays, LSD is an entertainment: bright colours and funny illusions at best. Now is not a time for dreams; now is a time for hedonism and escape. Reality is all too brutal and unavoidable. The reasons for this are manifold: society has changed; we are in a new economic situation; street 'acid' is much weaker than before; and we now understand just how truly the experience of LSD is governed by individual factors and thought processes.

So what is the LSD experience? What is it that led a generation to believe in the power of this chemical?

LSD nowadays comes in tabs (small, patterned squares of paper impregnated with the drug) and microdots (tiny tablets). In the 1960s, a standard street dose contained around 50 micrograms of LSD. About 100 micrograms will produce a full-blown hallucinatory event. Today's tabs contain on average 50–70 micrograms, although microdots are somewhat stronger. The tab or microdot is swallowed and what happens next depends on a combination of dosage, individual personality and mood, company and setting. LSD is an intensely personal experience, for reasons which will be explained later, but in broad terms it follows a clearly identifiable pattern.

Before we describe this experience, let us look at what is known about the drug's *modus operandi*: how it affects the body and brain. Levels of the drug in the body at different times following consumption are essentially unconnected to the nature and the strength of the experience at those times. Peak levels in body organs are reached about 15–20 minutes after consumption – before any visual effects even begin – although the peak in the small intestine is reached after two hours. Most of the LSD concentrates in the liver, with the smallest concentration being in the brain (the place where it has maximum effect). In the brain, maximum concentrations are found in the areas that interpret vision and in the emotional centres. LSD is metabolized very quickly, with blood levels halving every three hours and with the whole dose excreted within 24 hours. Given its slow start and long duration of effect, it is assumed that LSD must upset some natural system within the brain rather than act directly itself to cause perceptual change. What system it upsets and the mechanism for this is still not understood. We know that dopamine and serotonin are the neurotransmitters affected, but we don't know how. We know that LSD increases the size of sensory signals sent to the cortex and that electrocardiograms show arousal of this area, but little more is known.

It would take at least a 300 times overdose of LSD to kill. Tolerance to the drug's effects in users is spectacular. After three or four days, the same dose ceases to have any effect. This tolerance drops rapidly with abstinence; a few days off puts tolerance back to its original level. It is thus extremely difficult to develop a dependence on LSD – a strong liking maybe, but not a dependence.

Curiouser and curiouser

The experience of tripping, given a sufficiently high dose, seems to progress through four distinct, although merging and overlapping stages. In stage 1, so little actually happens that first-time users can think the drug hasn't worked and, to their later cost, take more. The effects of stage 1 are not psychedelic or hallucinatory; they are physical and subtle. For about 30–45 minutes the only measurable changes are a slight increase in body temperature, dilated pupils, a slight increase in blood pressure and heart rate, and an increase in sugar and saliva levels. These may be accompanied by minor sweats or chills, blurred vision, shakes, goose bumps and nausea. Most users don't notice these effects at all. The reason for them is unclear, but one possibility is that the user, who is only too aware of the unpredictability of the coming experience, is in a state of nervous expectation and that it is this state, rather than the drug itself, which causes the effects.

Stage 2 of the trip gradually introduces the main psychedelic effects. Sensory perception is intensified and altered. It is not, as is commonly understood, just vision which is affected, but all five senses. Visually, colours are intensified until they appear almost to burn into the retina: colours may smear (as when one looks at a bright light and then turns away) and after-images may be seen as in rapid still-frame photography of moving objects. These effects are known as 'traces' and 'tracking'. Sounds are intensified and register disproportionately. Smell, taste and touch are all altered. It is as though the senses are overloaded, or as if filters have been removed from our perception of external experience. Sometimes a kind of sensory cross-transference may occur, where messages from one sense are registered by another sense: users may 'see' sounds or 'hear' colours. The world seems to burst into overwhelming intensity.

But it is not just the senses that are affected in stage 2. Our appreciation of the passage of time is also greatly distorted. This is difficult to describe to non-users of LSD. Perhaps the easiest way to think of it is to think about how time seems to fly when we are happy and crawl by when we are bored. LSD magnifies such changes in the flow of time, so that a second may seem like minutes, packed with incident and emotion, and minutes can seem to pass in the blinking of an eye. In this timeless state, emotions take on new and overwhelming importance: they become exaggerated and wash through the user's perception in a way that is both overwhelming and at the same time distant or depersonalized. Stage 2 sometimes seems like watching the world as if it were a film.

With today's street doses, this is often as intense as it gets. While powerful, this is still a relatively manageable experience, ideal for the hedonistic user, but ultimately unsatisfying for the seeker of mysteries. Hallucinations at this stage fall into the category of illusion (seeing things which exist, but in distorted form) or pseudohallucinations (where users knows that they are imagining the things they see).

Stage 3 throws the user into Alice in Wonderland. Stage 2 may last for around an hour and a half before things move up a gear, but it is in stage 3 that the real LSD experience takes place. Pseudo-hallucinations and illusions are replaced by true hallucinations, where things are experienced which do not exist, or things which do exist are not registered. The user believes the experience, unable to tell what is real and what is not. This stage is significantly different because it seems to be controlled by the release of personal material, stored memories and emotional changes of an apocalyptic nature. The user's ideas seem overwhelmingly important and actually affect what is experienced. Trivial thoughts may be translated into hallucinatory reality, often in a caricature or cartoon-like reality: think of a police car and the person next to you develops a blue flashing light on her head; think about the vastness of existence and multicoloured translucent winds may sweep across huge empty spaces, only interrupted by trees grasping their leaf hands to the sky.

Another feature of stage 3 is ego-death: loss of body, self and control over behaviour, plus depersonalization. 'Self' can provoke 'bad trips'. At the same time, the emotional intensity reaches new levels. Mood changes may be rapid and overwhelmingly intense, from horror to a sense of calm oneness with the cosmos and back in a few moments. Against this background, the power of the mind to alter experience in a way which convinces users that what they are experiencing is reality indicates just what a perilous experience tripping can be.

If what you think happens, and you have no control over what you think because you have lost all concept of self, are swamped by emotion and are reacting to what you see, then you have to hope that what you think is pleasant. Think something unpleasant, experience something unpleasant; think something nastier, experience something horrific. LSD can be hell, and there's no getting off halfway through. Panicking because the trip won't stop can only make matters worse.

In the case of a bad trip, there is only one solution. Someone has to put pleasant thoughts back in your mind. Users on a bad trip need calm people who know how to 'talk them down' from the nightmare. It's no good someone saying 'I'll be over in a couple of hours' when time has become a totally flexible and infinitely stretchable concept. Talk to them calmly about things they'll enjoy. If they've got to finish the trip, let them at least finish it in style. Bright light helps: it is in the shadowy corners of rooms that children imagine monsters, and so it is with LSD. If the user wants to walk, let them. If they want to sit down, let them. Force does not work on bad trips; it just makes things worse. Bad trips can have long-lasting consequences for trippers, about which more later.

Stage 4, which may begin anywhere from four to six hours after ingestion of LSD, is the 'comedown'. LSD does not let the user glide smoothly back to earth. It is more a series of steps. Periodically, the individual may suddenly feel 'It's over now, I'm normal'; only to find that they are some way off. This kind of roller-coaster comedown can, in itself, be frightening because it may seem interminable, as though the user will never again get back to where they started. Usually, after eight to twelve hours the psychedelic effects are over. The very last part of the acid effect fading away is often a time of reflection or introspection, where the individual seeks to make sense of the enormity of what has just happened. Serious-minded trippers may use this time to reflect anew on their personality, or to create mythical constructs for their experience.

For a day or so after the trip, reality may seem as drab and flat as the world of LSD was spectacular, but for most users there are no harmful long-term effects. However, after an experience as mighty and intense as tripping, nobody truly comes back to the starting point. At the very least they are aware, albeit unconsciously, that reality is largely a matter of interpretation, that they themselves are in some way responsible for it, that reality is subjective, not objective. LSD at full doses changes those who take it in a subtle but long-lasting way.

On a bummer

For some individuals, about one in a thousand, the aftermath is more serious. Bad trips can cause a range of serious problems, from suicide, through lengthy to permanent psychoses, although more people are likely to suffer from lower-order 'mental' problems, such as loss of confidence (where do you turn when it is 'you' who have created an unpleasant reality?), emotional instability (a kind of jitteriness related to a loss of faith in the predictability of emotions and your capacity to deal with them) and depression.

There are predictors of who is most likely to have a bad trip and a lasting psychotic reaction. While for most users a bad trip is likely to be caused by mood, company, setting or events occurring during the trip, or by taking an unusually high dose, for others there are predisposing factors which make not only bad trips but also lasting reactions more likely. The prime example of an individual who should not take acid is someone with a predisposition to mental illness, particularly schizophrenia, as LSD can bring the whole illness on. If someone has blood relatives who have suffered from mental illness, or who have themselves suffered previously, taking acid is an enormous risk. Others at risk include insecure, unstable or immature personality types, paranoid or depressed individuals, and those with rigid personalities who like to see life ordered, in set routines and following clear rules – LSD just tears up the rule book.

There are two other group especially at risk of lasting reaction. The first is the inadvertent user: the individual who has been 'slipped a tab' in their drink without knowing. To be plunged into a psychedelic experience with no warning and against your will, with no chance to make mental preparations, can be particularly terrifying. How are you to interpret what is happening to you? Are you going mad? Why did this start and will it ever stop?

The last group at high risk is the high-dose, regular, long-term user. There is no way you can stare into the gates of heaven and hell repeatedly over a long period of time without damage to the psyche. With users in this group, it is almost possible to watch their personality disintegrate as time goes by. Usually the confidence goes first, then the paranoia arrives, followed by the psychosis. Perhaps the best example of an individual in this latter group from the world of popular culture is the guitarist Peter Green of Fleetwood Mac. LSD took him from being an outstandingly sensitive guitar player, through a brief burst of creative songwriting genius, to psychotic illness over a couple of years. Following a spell as a gravedigger, Peter grew his fingernails extraordinarily long so that he could not play the guitar and return to 'the Devil's work'. It is only now, some twenty-five years later, that he is showing signs of a return to health. Was there a predisposition? Peter puts it down to 'too much acid'.

The most disturbing case I have worked with personally was that of a 13-year-old boy who never touched down from his first trip. Months later, and after three hospital stays, he was still suffering from 'traces' and 'tracking' and strange noises. He was one of the unlucky ones. Most acid casualties return to normality after a few weeks or months, usually with treatment but sometimes naturally.

One of the most publicized phenomena associated with LSD is the 'flashback'. A flashback is a sudden, unexpected recurrence of the LSD experience sometimes months after last use. Flashbacks may occur only once or may be frequent, and may last from a few seconds to several hours. Most users do not seem to get unduly worried by flashbacks, but for some they can be deeply disturbing. No one is sure what causes them. Many seem to be sparked off by cannabis use. It seems likely that in such cases the tetrahydro-cannabinol (THC) in the cannabis reminds the user of the hallucinogenic experience. Thus, although smoking cannabis will never get them to a state of tripping, it is sufficient to make the users feel that that is where they may be going, mentally unprepared. The resulting mixture of panic and being 'stoned' may approximate to a feeling of tripping and be misinterpreted by the person concerned. It is common for people who have had a bad experience with LSD to turn to cannabis to relax them, only to find that as well as the sedative cannabinoid effect they also get the hallucinatory edge of the THC. We always advise against cannabis use for those getting over psychotic reactions to any drug because of the paranoia it can create.

However, not all those experiencing flashbacks get them during or following cannabis use. For such cases there have been a huge variety of theories, none of them ultimately satisfying. Those who experience flashbacks just have to hope they are not doing 90 mph on the motorway when the lamp-posts bend down and say hello!

Another well-publicized aspect of LSD is the 'flying' phenomenon. The idea that users think they can fly and hence jump off tall buildings has become something of a modern myth. Incidences are very rare in reality and yet everybody knows someone who has tried it. There is, nonetheless, a great deal of truth in the basic premise that LSD makes you think things are possible when they're not, and that you are capable of doing things that you can't. This could involve anything from thinking you have become so light that you can only walk on water, to thinking that you can walk straight across the road because fluffy balls can't run you over, even if they're travelling fast. Hallucinations cause false judgement and thus accidents. Don't even *think* that you'll be able to drive: you may make it, but I don't want to be on your stretch of road when you find out.

LSD users can also be a liability because they can bore you to death with endless detailed descriptions of their tripping exploits. It is hardly surprising, given the nature of the drug and the intensity of the experiences, that detailed memories of trips can last for decades. This is a powerful drug; the most powerful illegal drug commonly available in terms of effect and duration against weight.

No other drug could, for £2.50, give twelve hours of effect for 100 thousandths of a gram. In fact, given its cheapness, it is amazing that so few people take it. But then who can regularly take twelve hours out of a weekend to experience it, followed by 24–48 hours' recuperation, and still have a life?

Own goals

The reason for LSD's cheapness is, in itself, a lesson to be learned about the war on drugs. By the early 1970s there was a glut of high-grade, low-price LSD on the UK market. Nearly all of this turns out to have been manufactured by a former chemistry student, Richard Kemp, who had found a cheap and easy method of manufacture. The police mounted a huge undercover operation aimed at taking out most of the LSD in the UK in one swoop. The ensuing raid in 1974, codenamed Operation Julie, was hailed as a great success, and indeed supplies of acid in the UK all but dried up for several years. But if Kemp's arrest saw the end of one acid era, his trial in 1977 saw the birth of a new one. The court demanded that Kemp reveal his formula, which thus was placed on the public records of the trial and made available to anyone interested. Many obviously were, because by the early 1980s acid was back, and despite a few dips and rises in supply and demand, it hasn't gone away since.

Only the grin was left

Today, LSD seems to create few headlines, especially when viewed in relation to a media hungry for drug sensationalism. It barely rates a subheading compared to the banner headlines created by ecstasy or crack. It is not even top priority for the agencies of law enforcement. So what has changed? The answer seems to be that the health risks presented by the drug, serious though they are for some individuals, are not in themselves enough for authority and media attention when stripped away from the drug's political connotations. This is the real revelation of LSD and it is true of most drugs. Most illegal drugs kill very few people when compared to legal ones or even to 'soft' drugs like cannabis. Death is obviously not the issue. We are not being protected from dying. So why the hysteria and clampdowns on particular drugs at particular times? Because of the threat, real or perceived, that they represent to social codes and institutions, and because they can be used as a weapon with which to attack particular groups seen to be threatening the status quo.

Ecstasy is attacked not because of its dangers to health, but because of who takes it and what they represent. 'E' culture represents a turning away from the Protestant work ethic towards unbridled hedonism, away from family values towards a free-for-all. Its more extreme users, such as travellers, offend traditional values and, through association with drugs, can be portrayed as crazy, irresponsible and undesirable. Then you can clamp down. Crack is undoubtedly a nasty substance, but no worse than heroin or solvents, which no longer grab the headlines. Why the focus on crack? Because it has been consciously painted as a black drug. It creates the stereotype of the black gangster, marginalizing black people and taking the sting out of the claims for social justice. Crack, rather than racism and economics, can be conveniently blamed for black poverty and unemployment.

We've been here before. In the early 1980s, with recession (whatever happened to depression?) and escalating youth unemployment, the focus was on heroin. Yes, heroin was a problem, but it was just one more symptom of a social sickness, not its cause. It's easier to blame the symptom and divert attention from underlying problems. Will it be solvents or some other drug that becomes the focus for the breakdown of discipline among the young, for increasing levels of violence and the decline of morality?

In the 1960s, LSD was a problem not because it was killing people or frying young minds. The authorities were doing that in any case. Governments couldn't really have been concerned about a few LSD deaths compared to the daily death toll on the roads, or from nicotine-related lung cancer, or from alcohol-related illnesses, or from various 'small' wars. Governments were concerned about

LSD because it looked for a while as though it was about to reveal to a whole generation what was going on; it was going to undermine social values; it was used by those 'peaceniks' who opposed the Vietnam War. Shut LSD down and at the same time you were shutting down the real political opposition. And in the late 1960s and early 1970s, it actually began to look and act like a real political opposition.

Did acid really reveal truths about the way society is run and controlled? Was it really a threat to traditional moral values? Maybe, but probably not. It was more a symptom, a happy coincidence, of what was going on: social upheaval, change, a world entering the computer age, the 'white heat of the technological revolution'. But you could present the ideas of anyone who took it as crazy and dangerous, and you could arrest them for it.

If, on one level, LSD shows us the drugs issue as a focus for social control or a battlefield of ideologies, it also reveals something else about the way we live. In any other culture through history, LSD would have been revered. And I don't mean worshipped as an ultimate answer, in the naive and recklessly experimental fashion of 1960s youth culture; that is not reverence, which involves humility, but spiritual greed, spiritual materialism. Other cultures would have been in awe of the potential of this drug, of its magical powers, and would have developed structures over thousands of years with which to control its use (without the use of laws), while making use of its qualities and revelations. This is because the cultures of which I speak still had religious or spiritual values as a living force, which could place hallucinatory substances in a spiritual and moral framework which gave them meaning. The LSD experience, like that of other psychedelics before it, would have been given a context in which the visions it produced were harnessed and directed for means of enlightenment.

Instead, it arrived in the West, in a religious vacuum where revelatory experience was, at best, suspect. There was no framework of religious ideas for LSD to illuminate. Instead we created them as we went along, believing any revelatory experience to be divine in itself, any revelation to be better than none. But this free-form revelation had no meaning, or a million meanings; as many meanings as we could make up or as the next guru told us. LSD became a kind of spiritual package tour, six cities in a week, six metaphysical insights in twelve hours.

Together alone

And that finally is the crux of the problem with drugs. We in the West are in a godless universe, alone and scared of death, defining our worth by our possessions and grasping at straws. Here we find a garden of earthly (or heavenly) delights, in the form of an ever-expanding array of substances to which we turn to become the people we wish we were, or for the answers to questions when we're not even sure what the questions are. Like children in the sweet shop, we want some of everything. We pig out and feel sick, not really nourished. Speed or cocaine to be that sharp, confident go-getter we've always wanted to be, because that's what the world wants. LSD or mushrooms for a quick spiritual fix or just for a brief escape into fairyland. Solvents or heroin to hide the emptiness and pain.

For, just as the reaction of the authorities to drugs is ridiculously distorting and amoral, so is most individual use. Much of youth culture now seems to be saying of drug use, 'Ah, sod it. Why not get off your face? It only hurts the unlucky few. There are no real consequences.' The truth is that drugs do affect people, from individuals to whole economies across the globe. They enable us both as individuals and collectively to believe in easy instant solutions, rather than working problems through and fighting for change. They divide us from each other and cut us off from ourselves. They allow us to avoid looking at the spiritual void, the materialistic abyss, into which we are plunging. Treat drugs like just another commodity, with no respect, and they prove the master. Ultimately, if we cannot find the social and spiritual framework into which to place drugs and their use, then we are left with no alternative but to control them.

Coda – and in the end

Drug use is an immensely complex phenomenon and there are no easy answers, even if we could decide exactly what the questions are. Let me pose just a few questions of my own. There are many others.

- Do we want the right to put inside ourselves whatever chemicals we choose?
- Do we want to legalize the use of chemicals with harmful side effects, which alter our mood or perceptions, while restricting the sale of medicines with similar side effects, but which do not alter our mood or perceptions?
- Do we do more harm than good by criminalizing drug users?
- Do we think that legalizing drugs would aid or damage the economic well-being of those living in producer countries?
- How many civil liberties are we prepared to see eroded in the name of the war against drugs?
- Who stands to gain or lose from the current prohibition of drugs, or their legalization?
- If we are so concerned about helping the young, why do we spend our time covering our backs and playing with respectability instead of doing what works?
- Since contract culture, competitive tendering, etc., do those in the drug field work together more or less effectively in developing services for drug users of all ages?
- What would happen if the money from the drugs trade were taken out of the global economy?

These are just a few items for us all to ponder as we look ahead to the new millennium.

A conclusion? As if! This one is going to run and run.

Useful addresses

Newham Drugs Advice Project (NDAP)
Abbey House
361 Barking Road
Plaistow
London E13 8EE
tel. 0171-474 2222

Dorset Youth Awareness Programme
39 Easton Street
Portland
Dorset DT5 1BF
tel. 01305 823823

Haringey and Enfield Youth Awareness Programme
Selby Centre
Selby Road
Tottenham
London N17 8JN
tel. 0181-493 9000

Merton Youth Awareness Programme
226 London Road
Mitcham
Surrey CR4 3HD
tel. 0181-648 3682

Newham Youth Awareness Programme
Abbey House
361 Barking Road
Plaistow
London E13 8EE
  tel. 0171-474 2222

Sutton Youth Awareness Programme
103 Westmead Road
Sutton
Surrey SM1 4JD
  tel. 0181-770 0017

Central Drugs Co-ordinating Unit
Room 354
Horseferry House
Dean Ryle Street
London SW1P 2AW
  tel. 0171-217 8631

Institute for the Study of Drug Dependence (ISDD)
Waterbridge House
32–36 Loman Street
London SE1 0EE
  tel. 0171-928 1211

Release
388 Old Street
London EC1V 9LT
  tel. 0171-729 9904

Standing Conference on Drug Abuse (SCODA)
Waterbridge House
32–36 Loman Street
London SE1 0EE
  tel. 0171-928 9500

A full list of drugs agencies is available from SCODA at the address
above.

Index

ISSUES IN SOCIAL POLICY

The approach of the Issues in Social Policy series is both academically rigorous and accessible to the general reader. The authors are well known and active in their fields.

Nudes, Prudes and Attitudes: Pornography and censorship
Avedon Carol

Shortlisted for the Women in Publishing Pandora Award

Pornography and censorship have carved a divide in the feminist movement and beyond. On one side is an improbable alliance of pro-censorship feminists – most famously Catharine MacKinnon and Andrea Dworkin – and the moral right. On the other are civil libertarians of various shades and anti-censorship feminists.

This is the only UK-based single-author account of the pornography debate from a feminist perspective. It argues strongly that the movement for sexual censorship gives enormous and dangerous powers to the state, promotes the very repression that is implicated in causing sexual violence, and derails feminist discussion of sexuality and related vital issues.

Nudes, Prudes and Attitudes is essential reading for students of women's studies, media studies, sociology, psychology and government, and will be of interest to all those concerned with the civil liberties implications of censorship.

Avedon Carol is a feminist, an activist and a member of Feminists Against Censorship. She is co-editor of *Bad Girls and Dirty Pictures: The challenge to reclaim feminism.*

'a stimulating read' *New Humanist*

'a provocative and challenging book' *Gay and Lesbian Humanist*

'an important statement on the modern feminist stand against the horrors of censorship' *Desire*

'sets out clear and reasoned responses to all the arguments commonly trotted out against pornography' *SKIN TWO*

'What impresses me most about the book is the combination of personal experience, contemporary cultural commentary and historical analysis ... If you only read one book about the crippling dispute among feminists over pornography and censorship, make *Nudes, Prudes and Attitudes* that book.'
Dr William Thompson, *New Times*

---

224 pages, illustrated
Paperback   £11.95   ISBN 1 873797 13 3
Hardback   £25.00   ISBN 1 873797 14 1

Domestic Violence: Action for change
Gill Hague and Ellen Malos

Male violence against women in the home is in the public eye as never before. One of the commonest crimes, it is present throughout society. In any house, on any average street, women regularly experience abuse and violence.

This widely acclaimed study covers the full range of domestic violence issues. It explains clearly what domestic violence is, gives a concise history of the refuge movement and examines a range of explanations for male violence against women. The book charts recent changes in policing, the law, housing, the caring professions and inter-agency initiatives, and highlights the need to change social attitudes through public education and campaigning.

Written in close co-operation with the Women's Aid federations and the refuge movement, this is an accessible and comprehensive account of the domestic violence issue both for practitioners and for students of social work, social policy, sociology and women's studies.

Gill Hague and Ellen Malos are researchers into domestic violence at the University of Bristol and campaigners on domestic violence issues. Ellen Malos is also the editor of *The Politics of Housework*, now newly republished by New Clarion Press.

'An extremely useful and welcome addition to the literature on woman abuse ... a basic resource for activists and practitioners which provides a comprehensive summary of current perspectives and developments in the field of domestic violence.' Nicola Harwin, National Co-ordinator, Women's Aid Federation England.

'likely to be of value to students, researchers, practitioners and academics ... should be widely read and the findings disseminated' *British Journal of Social Work*

'If you have ever wondered who said what when about woman abuse, this book will provide the source ... well worth having' *Scottish Women's Aid Newsletter*

'The strength of the book is in the coverage of recent changes ... reflects insights based on a familiarity with the issue of battering' Rebecca Emerson Dobash, *Community Care*

---

240 pages, illustrated
Paperback   £11.95   ISBN 1 873797 06 0

A second edition in paperback and hardback will be published in 1998.

Antibody Politic: AIDS and society
Tamsin Wilton

The global AIDS epidemic that appeared in the 1980s brought with it a social epidemic: the fear, hatred, bigotry, denial and repression with which the peoples of the world have reacted. The way we, as a society, respond to AIDS is an acid test of our values, our humanity and our social policy.

This book discusses the issues raised by AIDS for every member of society. It outlines concisely the history of the epidemic to date and summarizes concisely the basic medical information on HIV and AIDS. It then considers AIDS in relation to the gay community, to women and to minority ethnic groups, and analyses its policy implications. From an account of community responses to the epidemic, and of the problematic relationship between the state and voluntary sectors, the book moves to a construction of the probable future and recommendations for personal and political action.

Tamsin Wilton lectures in health studies and women's studies at the University of the West of England, Bristol. Her publications include *AIDS: Setting a feminist agenda* and *En/Gendering AIDS*.

'This useful book explains what HIV infection is, how you can get it and how not to. It might also help you to decide what you think should be done about it.' *Guardian*

'an invaluable guide ... a must for students from a variety of disciplines' *AIDSLINK*

'particularly interesting to those who are looking for a feminist perspective on the AIDS epidemic' American Library Association

'a recommended book ... deserves a place in all academic and medical libraries' *AIDS Book Review Journal*

'an accessible yet sophisticated analysis ... an extremely valuable resource' Lesley Doyal, Professor of Health Studies, University of the West of England

176 pages, illustrated
Paperback   £9.95   ISBN 1 873797 04 4
Hardback   £25.00   ISBN 1 873797 05 2

For more information on books published by New Clarion Press:
New Clarion Press, 5 Church Row, Gretton, Cheltenham GL54 5HG
tel./fax 01242 620623